Tayto, Tea and Slimming World.

GW00394251

I look for the beauty in the banal.
I look for the majesty in the mundane.

By Don Clampet.
2017
(not my real name)

Saturday, 5 November 2011
Why does my hair look so grey on me head, but have a luscious brown sheen on the barbers floor?

Monday, 7 November 2011
I'm in trouble.
I was in the shower.
I got soap in my eyes.
I reached out for a towel to clean it off.
I lifted the decorative not to be used towel.
I may have to go on the run.

Monday, 5 December 2011
I had a spell in the Royal Victoria Hospital a few years ago.
I was beside an older gentleman.
He asked to speak to the doctor one day.
The doctor came in and pulled the curtains round the cubicle.
I could hear every word, but there was nothing I could do about it.
The wife did most of the talking.
He is worried about the nurses she said.
What about the nurse's Dr said.
He doesn't like some of them she said.
Why not Dr said.
He thinks the two Filipino ones are going to rob him she said.
They are two excellent nurses Dr said.
He doesn't want them touching him she said.
He doesn't want them anywhere near him she said.
He is refusing to be treated by them she said.
He is not a racist Doctor but he can't understand them and he doesn't trust them she said.
He wants nurses that speak English she said.
Have they done anything specific Dr asked.
Not yet, but they will she said.
They will she said again ominously.
OK Dr said.
Leave it with me Dr said.
I will be back shortly.
He left.

I was astounded. I was angry, I was livid, I was furious.

I couldn't believe what I was hearing. I resolved to register my complete and utter disgust at racism like this.

The doctor returned 10 minutes later.
He pulled the curtains closed again.
Now sorry for the delay Dr says.
These are your release papers Dr says.
These will let you go home Dr says.
You can take these to your GP Dr says.
He will send you to another hospital where you will hopefully be more comfortable Dr says.
Of course, you will unfortunately return to the end of the queue Dr says.
That can't be helped, as you have refused treatment here Dr says.
Well cheerio then Dr says.
Take care Dr says.
And off he went.
The next cubicle was stunned into silence.

He came straight in to me as the next patient.
And how are you today Dr says?
Mighty doctor, says me with a big goofy grin. I'm feckin mighty.

Tuesday, 31 January 2012
The lady behind the counter in Victoria Road post office is called Marina.
The gentleman she is serving is called Maurice.
I'm finding this very amusing.

Friday, 2 March 2012
I'm in B&Q at Hollywood Exchange.
I'm buying grout.
I selected a tub.
I opened it to see if there was a grout spreader inside.
There was a spreader inside.
A worker came up to me.
He seemed upset.
He seemed a bit aggressive.
You're not allowed to open that he says.
Really says me?
It goes off if you open it he says.
OK says me.
I put the pot back on the shelf and lifted a different one.
Are you not taking that one he says, pointing at the one I had left back on the shelf.

No says me, that one's been opened.
It goes off apparently.

We then went to IKEA.
There is a stand on the way in.
There are pictures of bears and leopards on the stand.
An earnest young lady comes up to me.
She stands right in front of me and blocks the way.
I immediately dislike her.
Hello sir she says.
Are you interested in local wildlife she says abrasively?
She is standing in my personal space.
Yes, I am says me.
I certainly am says me.
I go hunting every weekend says me.

Why are people getting cross with me today?

Tuesday, 6 March 2012
I went for a walk last night.
I'm trying to be good.
I went past the Brown Cow Inn, no problems there.
The Rugby club was nearly empty, still no problems.
Further down Woodburn Road I passed Dominos, the Chinese, the chippy, and the Indian.
I was starting to wilt.
I had to cross over the road because there is no footpath on my side.
That put me now on the same side as the Moghul.
I like the Moghul.
The Moghul likes me.
I crossed back immediately after the bridge but before I reached the Moghul, drooling.
I kept my head down passing the Moghul.
I felt embarrassed.
I felt I had let them down.
I went past Gods house.
It came just at the right time for me.
Bless me father for I have sinned.
I disowned the Moghul, just like St Peter disowned Jesus.
Walk on my child.
Munchies and another Chinese are on the other side of the road. They didn't even tempt me.
I have it beat now I thought.

I'm laughing now I thought.
This walking crack is easy I thought.
I was at the bottom of the hill.
I turned the corner onto Shore Road.
I was the Golden Arches.
I forgot about the Golden Arches, sure one strawberry milkshake wouldn't hurt.
But it was on the wrong side of the road so I kept going.
Next block housed the Indian Ocean, Dragon Inn, and KFC.
Galway girl came on the playlist just in time, I skipped and sang along and kept going.
There were blue flashing lights coming fast behind me.
Oh my God, someone saw the state of me and called an ambulance.
It wasn't an ambulance.
It was the Police.
Oh my God, someone saw the state of me and called the police.
They didn't stop.
I came to Trooperslane.
It's a pull uphill to the railway level crossing.
Every time I drive up a train comes and blocks it for 10 minutes.
I was ready for the train and a nice wee rest.
I resolved to lean on the barrier, but to let go when the barrier started to rise.
There was no train, I had to keep going.
I'm going to write a stiff letter of complaint to Ciaran Rogan off Translink.
I turned onto Top Road heading for home.
I wheezed and breezed past the beautifully floodlit building in the foothills that is the water treatment plant.
I made it home.
Quick lads phone the Chinese I'm dying.

Friday, 18 May 2012
I was chatting to an acquaintance.
I asked after the kids.
The eldest boy is working now he says.
He works for a lovely man.
He serves customers and works the till and everything.
The boss leaves him in charge while he goes to the cash and carry.
You should go to the shop, he can get you stuff for free.
He does it all the time for us.

If the boss is such a lovely man, says me, why is your son stealing from him?

Silence.

Friday, 27 July 2012

Wee daughter, Lauren, Linda and a few others were going out on the jet skis at Fisherman's Quay. They had the donut out, towing the kids behind the jet ski.

I had to have a go. I waded in in my shorts and t-shirt.

Off Mervyn went with me clinging to the back, bouncing happily along.

It was great fun.

We were flying round when I started to feel my shorts slipping.

I could feel them getting dragged downwards.

The water passing by underneath was dragging them backwards.

I tried to grab them, but I wouldn't manage to stay on the donut one handed.

I opened my legs wide so that they wouldn't go very far.

They would only go to thigh level, or worst case knee level.

I flew round the harbour, hanging on for dear life, bouncing over the wake with my legs wide open and my shorts down.

I managed to stay on the donut.

The shorts unfortunately did not.

I had to stay in the water with my t-shirt tucked between my legs until the shorts could be recovered.

Linda asked what was wrong.

I explained that I had parted company with my shorts.

Thanks to Mervyn for recovering the offending articles much to the enjoyment of Linda, and the embarrassment of Lauren.

It's surprisingly awkward to put on your shorts in the waves with one hand while holding your t-shirt down to protect your modesty in the other. Mervyn helped by splashing me repeatedly.

It was a cold evening. The water was very cold. Just remember that when the girls are telling you about it.

Friday, 24 August 2012

Mrs Brown has curly hair and glasses like my mammy.

Mrs Brown has four sons and a daughter like my mammy.

Mrs Browns eldest son is cool and in control like my mammy's eldest.

Mrs Browns youngest is a gangster like my mammy's.

Mrs Browns another son is a priest, and I was once a fancy-dress nun.

We all depend on our sister to keep us right.

We have a lanky camp brother.

MY MAMMY IS MRS BROWN!

Thursday, 6 September 2012

The Hells Bells doesn't like my motorbike.

Her pet name for it is that effin motorbike.
She had a puncture in her car.
She asked to borrow my car.
I had plans and needed the car.
So, she enquired whether I could possibly go on the bike.

She didn't say 'that effin motorbike'
She said 'the bike'.
It's like it's a part of the family.
It's like its accepted.
It's the bike.
I've had a smug smirk ever since.

Thursday, 13 September 2012

The wee motorbike gained a bit of acceptance last week.
And then yesterday I, in a vast overestimation of the quality and level of this grudging acceptance, hung the bike jacket over the banister.
All goodwill gained has now been lost.
The wee motorbike is now back to that effin motorbike.
Ah well.

Monday, 17 September 2012

I got my hair cut today.
It took 6 minutes to cut my hair, and then two mins more to trim my ears.
This worried me.
I did some research.
The average head has 100,000 hairs.
Purely on a time basis, I estimate that each of my ears has 16,667 hairs.
I have too much time on my hands.
I have too much hair in my ears.
I'm not getting my hair cut again.

Tuesday, 16 October 2012

Dear young miss in the Alfa.
You stopped in the middle of the road outside the school to talk to your friend.
That wasn't a nice thing to do.
You blocked the traffic.
That wasn't a nice thing to do.
The lady behind waited for a bit and then politely blew her horn to request you to move along or pull in and park.

You jumped out of the car, your face twisted with rage, you launched an expletive filled tirade at her.

That wasn't a nice thing to do.

Your hair is nicely set.

Your makeup looks tidy and well applied.

You are nicely and professionally dressed.

You are slim and appear fit.

But underneath it all you are an ugly f**ker.

Tuesday, 16 October 2012

Tuesdays are awkward.

Wee daughter gets out at 4.30, the Hells Bells picks her up. The Hells Bells finishes work in Belfast at 4, the same time as I do. She gets to the school at about 4.40, same as I would. However, if I take the effin bike I'm there at 4.25. So, the Hells Bells would like me to take the effin bike to Belfast on Tuesdays, ride home, then hop in the car and be at the school to get wee daughter on time. But the Hells Bells hates the effin bike so much she can't bring herself to ask.

So this morning she asked if I was going in on the bike.

No says me, it's a bit wet.

She thought about it. She looked out the window. She looked up at the sky. She checked the wind direction. She looked at the horizon.

It's to brighten up later on says she.

She couldn't look at me. She couldn't face me.

I was shocked. I was surprised. I was delighted. I tried vainly to keep my face straight.

I wanted to say no.

I wanted to tell her that she had ignored and insulted and nagged my wee motorbike for years.

I wanted to tell her that now she needed the wee motorbike, maybe the wee motorbike would respond in kind.

I wanted to rant and rave and moan and groan and huff and puff.

I didn't. I stood there with a sarcastic knowing smile.

We will see says me, sure I might.

Friday, 30 November 2012

What would you like for Xmas she asked?

Anything you like, just name it she said.

Well, says me thinking.

I would like a chrome tax disc holder for the motorbike says me

Apart from that she said.

Nothing to do with that effin motorbike she said.

Sunday, 2 December 2012
I go for a walk.
There is a vote tomorrow on removing the Union Flag from Belfast City Hall.
I count flags.
Just for the craic.
There is a Union Flag on the Orange Hall.
There is a Union Flag on the Belgian Arch.
There are 13 Union Flags outside the Catholic Church.
There is a Union Flag at the Town Hall.
There is a Union Flag on the War Memorial.

Make your own mind about that.
You decide if that is proper treatment of a National flag.

Tuesday, 4 December 2012
There was a flag protest riot in Belfast.
A barrier pushed over, a brick was thrown, 8 policemen went off on the sick.
Some grannies and teenagers broke a window and got into City Hall, but were
thwarted by double swing doors with no lock. They burned one National Flag in
protest of the insult to another National Flag.
It started to rain, so they went home.
The price of fuel precluded the use of petrol bombs.
8000 children and parents meanwhile went to the Odyssey to see JLS.
They were a bigger draw.

Thursday, 3 January 2013
I was walking out of the garage carrying a subway salad and a top shelf magazine,
when I bumped into a client.
I was so embarrassed.
Luckily, I managed to hide the salad behind my back, and she didn't see it.
Phew.

Saturday, 13 April 2013
I have discovered that when the satnav lady is speaking in my car I can turn her
down using the volume buttons.
I can turn her off using the mute button.
I wonder if it works on the Hells Bells.
Hells Bells, come here a wee sec.......

Saturday, 20 April 2013
So, the Hells Bells and me spent the afternoon riding.
The Hells Bells hasn't had a ride in years, but I've been riding a few times a week.
I'm actually getting quite good at it.
I normally do it alone, so it's nice to have company.
The Hells Bells held on to me for dear life, God bless her.
Don't worry, we had protection, and rode safely.
I was tempted to take her up the back road, but it can get very windy.
She may go riding again, or I may ride alone

on the motorbike.

Tuesday, 4 June 2013
I don't like to remind Ulster of their defeat to the mighty Leinster last week. But then Ulster's last victory in Leinster was in 1690, and they haven't shut up about it since.....

Wednesday, 10 July 2013
We are in Dargans Bar in Santa Barbara.
We are playing pool.
A young lady with her skirt above the knee at the next table commented on the auld brogue.
Ah Jaysus Howaye says me.
The Hells Bells sprang into action.
She marked her territory.
The young lady with skirt above the knee was put back in her cage.
Don't mess with the Hells Bells

Thursday, 11 July 2013
Agenda for tomorrow in Los Angeles.
1 Drop wife at shops.
2 Advise wife of baggage limits for flight home.
3 Be warned by wife to enjoy golf, but to warm up, so that I don't hurt the back.
4 Ignore wife and go golfing, don't warm up, cos we are in California.
5 Hurt back.
6 Collect wife with bags and bags.
7 Blame lifting all the shopping for sore back
8 Wife will blame the golf.

9 All will have a good day.

Sunday, 25 August 2013
I went up to the wee chippy van in the centre of Pettigo.
What can I get you she says?
Fish says me.
Fish she says?
Aye says me.
Oh, she says.
Oh, says me?
I don't think we have any she says.
Let me go see she says.
Keep an eye on the van she says.
And she left.
I stood there waiting at the empty van.
I felt like an eejit.
Then I went into the van.
That felt better.
I pulled on an apron.
That felt better again.
I started slicing some spuds.
That felt perfect.
So as of now I am now in charge of the chippy van in Pettigo if any of you are in the area. Just don't ask for fish.

She came back with a bag frozen Donegal Catch. She dumped two fillets straight in the fryer. I tasted them later. They were horrible.

The food was definitely better when I worked that van.

Friday, 30 August 2013
The Hells Bells and myself were walking across the Odyssey car park.
It started to rain.
Oh no says HB.
It's starting to rain says HB.
If my white top gets wet it gets see through says HB.
My heart skipped skipped skipped a beat.

Then she found an umbrella in her handbag.
I hate umbrellas.
I hate handbags.

Monday, 2 September 2013
So anyway after 12 years of driving the kids to school every morning big son drove wee daughter this morning.
I was left redundant, and beyond use.
You would think that I would be happy with this development.
I thought I would be happy with this development.
But I am not.
I am sad that the kids are grownupish.
I am sad that I am surplus.
Like an appendix.
Appendix dad.

Monday, 9 September 2013
I love the Dublin humour.
It's hard and merciless, but witty and funny.
I was driving on the South Side of the river.
I was looking for the car park in Fleet Street in Temple Bar.
I wasn't rushing to find it.
I wasn't under pressure to find it.
I was happy just to wander in that general direction.
The one-way system was messing with me. I was out near Christ Church.

I passed two Guards on horseback.
I pulled in to ask directions.
I approached cautiously.
Excuse me Guard says me.
Yes sir he says.
The horse whinnied.
The horse threw his head up and down.
I was keeping an eye on the horse.
The horse didn't seem to like me.
Could you tell me the way to Fleet Street says me, still keeping a watch on the horse?
You needn't be asking him the Guard says.
He is a country horse the Guard says.
He is grand in Mayo he says.
But he hasn't a clue round here he says.
The horse whinnied in agreement.
Dublin humour. Merciless but funny.

Monday, 23 September 2013

I was at mass in Carrick for a Month's Mind memorial service.
The priest greeted us and thanked us as we left.
He shook my hand.
He didn't let go.
Thanks for coming he says.
No bother Father says me.
We appreciate it he says.
No bother at all Father says me, gently pulling at my hand and trying to move away. He didn't let go.
No really, I know you are busy he says.
Family comes first Father says me.
And it's a long way for you to come isn't it says he.
No, sure I live up here now says me, worried that the crowd was building up behind us.
Do you he says.
Aye, just up the road says me.
Really? he says, still not releasing my hand.
Just up the road Father says me.
It's just I haven't seen you at Mass he says.
He released my hand with a wee satisfied smile.
I was pushed by the crowd out the door before I could reply.
Well played Father, well played.

Friday, 4 October 2013
Dear Hells Bells, we need to talk.
I went up to collect your mothers picture from the framers.
While I was there I made a purchase.
At this point I think it would be useful if you could vent the rage before you get home.
And remember technically it's all your mothers fault.
You should forgive her.

Friday, 4 October 2013
I was on the beer in Carrickfergus.
Just a nice night with a bit of devilment and a lot of craic.
I was propping up the bar at the end of the night when I was approached by two young ladies.
Scuze me they said.
Yes, says me.
We love Big Fat Gypsy Wedding they said.
Do you says me?
Yes, they said.

OK says me thinking that this was an odd conversation, even in my drunken state.
Can we ask you something they said?
Go ahead says me.
Are you here for a gypsy wedding they said?
I wanted to say no.
I wanted to say how dare they assume that I was a gypsy, despite me being a big, curly haired, English registered Mercedes driving, culchie accented lump of a lad.
I said yes.
I said yes I am.
The Hells Bells rolled her eyes. Then she rolled away.
It's on this Sunday says me.
In the church opposite Tesco at 12 says me.
Would you like to go says me?
Really, they said?
Really says me.
We would love to they said.
OK says me.
I will pick you up at Tesco at 12 says me.
You have seen the programme haven't you says me?
They nodded earnestly.
You know the dress code says me?
They nodded earnestly.
See you then says me.

There was some excitement in Carrick that weekend about the Big Fat Gypsy Wedding coming to town. It spiralled. It went viral. I kept my head down. We went out on Sunday. We avoided the church opposite Tesco. We took the back road out.

I was approached on the following Tuesday at work.
Were you on the beer in Carrick last week she says.
I was, yes says me.
How did you know says me?
I thought so she says.
I heard all about the big curly southerner in the English registered Mercedes inviting people to the gypsy wedding and I immediately thought of you she says.
I wanted to deny it.
I wanted to ask how dare she assume that I was the gypsy, despite me being a big, curly haired, English registered Mercedes driving, culchie accented lump of a lad.
But I said yes.
I said with a smile that was me.
She knew it was.

Tuesday, 8 October 2013

I'm sitting with my mammy watching Fair City.
My mammy was on a retreat with the nuns in Larne.
She escaped an hour ago.
No TV in the room apparently.
I picked her up at the gate.
I drove with lights off.
My mammy hid low down in the seat.
We were going to break for the border, but we reckon the nuns would have it covered.
If any nuns ask, you haven't heard from me.

Tuesday, 8 October 2013
Me mammy has handed herself in.
She may have gotten an amnesty from the nuns, or she may be in the punishment block overnight.
You can hide from the Police, the FBI and Interpol, but the no one messes with the Sisters of Mercy.

Thursday, 10 October 2013
I'm in Agnews Mercedes in Belfast.
My car is booked in for a service.
I've been waiting an hour just to leave the car.
No Agnews, I don't want tea.
Or coffee.
Or a wee shortbread.
I want you to just take my key and service my car, so I can go to work.
Please.
I will take a shortbread with me, if you insist.
And a cuppa, a small one.
But please take the car and start servicing it.

Thursday, 10 October 2013
Agnews have sensed my frustration at the delay, so they sent the young lady with cleavage over to cheer me up. I informed the cleavage that the delay was no problem whatsoever, and I apologised for putting the cleavage to bother. I could be here all day at this rate. The cleavage will be busy.

Thursday, 10 October 2013
The cleavage apologised again.
I told her chest that I wasn't happy at the delay.

She tried the old bending down trick.
I stood firm.
The cleavage ordered and paid for a taxi to Dundonald and back for me.
I thanked the cleavage.

Tuesday, 12 November 2013
So, the republicans are up in arms because the Sinn Fein Lord Mayor attended a Remembrance Day event. And the loyalists are up in arms because the Sinn Fein Lord Mayor attended a Remembrance Day event. When you think about it, the loyalists and republicans have so much in common, you would think they would get on with each other better........

Wednesday, 4 December 2013
Just been advised by a salesman that Siri is full of wit and whimsy.
I don't need it says me.
I've got friends for that.

Wednesday, 25 December 2013
Tensions were high in the house today.
The Hells Bells wanted to invite my clan up boxing day.
I was insistent on bringing them up St Stephens day.
Nanny Anne put a stop to the disagreement by deciding she would come to visit Thursday.
All parties are happy.
Richard Haas will be relieved.

Tuesday, 31 December 2013
Anyway, that's been 2013.
We have lost some real characters.
We have gained some new ones.
The St Declan's day campaign rolls on.
The Eurovision song contest song has stalled.
I've grown a moustache, badly.
I've played golf badly.
I've stayed on top of the effin bike.
I met and fell in love with Effin cheese.
I've sinned, venial sins only, not mortal, I think.
I've laughed a lot, punned a lot, worried about you lot.
I've watched people leave.
I've watched some come home.

I've watched some enjoying life away.
I've seen breakups and makeups.
And then breakups again.
Kids astound us, amaze us, frustrate the hell out of us.
I'm still crossing the North South Leinster Ulster divide.
Missus Brown isn't really my mammy.
I didn't lose weight.
I didn't stop picking on the Hells Bells.
I didn't stop effin.
So, last year's resolutions mostly failed.
On the plus side, I don't have to think of any new resolutions this year.
Nights in. Nights out. Nights in and out. Nights out and in.
The wife put up with me. The kids put up with me. Mrs Brown put up with me.
The friends put up with me. Samaritans told me to stop phoning.
I'm still scared of nuns and cleavages and Hyundai Getzes. Luckily, I have never come across all three together at the same time.
Great fun and laughs with nieces and nephews and adopted nieces and nephews.
McDonald's has taken a battering. Fish vans have taken a battering.
So that's it. I have genuinely enjoyed your company. Next year I hope u all laugh more than u cry, smile more than you frown, giggle wiggle and jiggle.
I'm off to work on my twerking. Happy new year.

Friday, 3 January 2014
Anyway, you know when you are out walking and you meet a gang of hoodies and they scare you and intimidate you so you cross the road to avoid them?
Out the end of the lane on one side is weight watchers.
Straight ahead is the funny church.
On the other side is the Orange hall.
I CAN'T CROSS THE ROAD PEOPLE THERE IS NO SAFE SIDE.
I'm done for.
As long as it's not weight watchers that get me.
Anything but weightwatchers.

Wednesday, 8 January 2014
Its new year's resolution time. I have decided that when I lose 2 stone myself and the Hells Bells are taking the effin bike to the Isle of Man, and we are going to go around the TT course. Its long been on the wish list. The Hells Bells has reacted by feeding me curry crisps and beer. It's just a win win for me.

Saturday, 18 January 2014
I was walking along Bridge Street in Belfast.

I was just passing the wee beggar woman when I heard the Samsung ring tone.
I pulled out my phone, shiny new Samsung S4, but it wasn't me ringing.
The beggar woman lifted shawl after shawl and eventually pulled out her phone,
also a shiny new Samsung S4.
She looked at me and smiled.
I smiled back because me and beggar woman are now phone buddies.
She shrugged as if to say 'bloody phones, can never get away from them'.
I shrugged back as if to say 'tell me about it'.
And off I went on my merry way.
Maybe to get a new phone.
Or possibly to take up begging.
There must be money in it.

Wednesday, 22 January 2014
The police are at the dissident Weightwatchers this morning.
About time I say.
I have put up with their intimidation, their bullying and their harassment.
A man should feel safe in his own shared lane.
Well done the PSNI.
Brave men.

Wednesday, 22 January 2014
The police have left.
They were clutching a wee folder each.
They were met at the door by a buxom hairy woman who relieved them of 50 quid
for membership and ordered them to surrender their weapons for the weighing.
Listen lads, whenever you are choosing a house don't worry about amenities, bus
runs, good schools and all that stuff, just make sure you stay well away from the
scourges that are Weightwatchers and Slimming World.

Saturday, 25 January 2014
A wee earnest survey volunteer came up to me and asked me to complete a survey
on the importance of religion in my life. She had 10 pre-planned things that may or
may not have been more important to me than religion e.g. family yes, friends yes,
health yes etc. And then she asked me anything else that I view as more important
to me than religion.
Well actually yes says me.
One or two things says me.
Do you want to jot them down says me?
Ok here go says me.
Painted on eyebrows. That's an important issue.

Effin bikes.
How do you spell effin she says.
EFFIN says me.
She wrote it down.
Getzes says me.
Hipsters.
Polly pockets.
Chinese restaurants not stocking Chinese beer.
Lads with trousers below their arse cheeks.
People calling me buddy in top road garage and asking do I want 4 KitKat for a quid.
Facebook. But not twitter. You can keep Twitter says me.
X factor but not Strictly.
St Declan's day and the lack of proper recognition.
Consubstantial, it has no place in the mass.
All very important things that rank highly in my life.
I think she was sorry she asked.
Section 2 was about the importance of nationality to me. She just left it blank.

Monday, 27 January 2014
Dear Newtownabbey Borough Council.
I'm sorry you felt the need to try to ban a play because it is about the bible. The play is now a massive sell out as a result.
My names Irish.
I like themuns.
I support gay pride.
And mothers pride.
I'm setting up grey pride.
I don't swim but if I did I would do it on a Sunday.
I don't shop but if I did I would do it on a Sunday.
I don't fancy Iris or Rhonda.
I'm too old for Iris, and I prefer Honda.
I like immigrants I sort of am one.
I like tattoos I sort of want one.
Brennans bread is nicer than Ormeau bread.
Red white and blue Tayto is nicer than the yellow Tandragee stuff.
Down south is nice.
Its warmer.
Its friendlier.
And they take sterling.
Except on the toll at Drogheda, that's Euro only. They do that just to annoy you.
GAA is good craic.
So is rugby.

I once bought a bootleg CD in Jonesborough.
I once bought red diesel in Pettigo.
I once filled up on green diesel cocktails in Erins Isle, Algarve.
I wear sandals and socks.
I once said North without the capital N.
I can only put up with 5 mins of gospel music before I slope off looking for the disco.
I once mistook the Sash for Sean South of Garryowen.
Or maybe it was vice versa.
Anyway, if you could ban me from Ballyearl golf range that would be much appreciated.
And please tell everyone about it.
God bless.

Wednesday, 29 January 2014
DW sports in Abbeycentre have moved the golf stuff. It used to be up the stairs and turn right. That area is now women's running. I was knee deep in sports bras and pink stuff before I realised. Be warned.

Wednesday, 5 February 2014
I took a call from a new client and we arranged to meet in Café Nero.
We had never met before.
I asked him what he looked like so I would know him.
Well he says, I'm very tall.
How tall says me?
6 2 he says.
That's not very tall says me.
Isn't it he says?
Not really says me.
I'm 6 1 and I'm not very tall says me.
I know he says but I'm 6 2. If I was 6 1 I would be tall, but I'm 6 2 so I'm very tall.
And then he said comprende?
I did my unimpressed sneer shrug, but as we were on the phone he didn't get the full benefit.
And I'm bald he says.
6 2 and bald in Belfast says me.
That doesn't narrow it down much says me.
Comprende? says me back to him, quite proud of myself for that one.
And I did the shrug again to reinforce the point.
And then he said ok and I'm black.

Could you not have imparted that crucial information at the start Sherlock?
Needless to say, I had no bother picking him out in Cafe Nero.
He was very tall.
Comprende?

Friday, 7 February 2014
I was at the motorbike show in Kings Hall.
I was chatting to a bike fabricator from Lurgan.
He stuck out his hand.
I'm Mick he says, everyone calls me Scallions.
Howaye Scallions says me.
I'm Don says me.
Everyone calls me…..

Then I realised I don't have a cool nickname.
The Hells Bells does call me Babes sometimes but I can hardly tell a huge biker called Scallions to call me Babes.
Or maybe I can but that could get me in more trouble.
Bike nickname.
My handle.
And then it dawned on me.
I deepened my voice.
Spoke with a drawl.
I'm Don says me.
Everyone calls me Effin says me.

I dragged an imaginary puff of a ciggie.
I narrowed my eyes and looked into the distance.
I was cool.
I was hard.
I was accepted.
We shook hands.
He said nice to meet you Ethan.

Wednesday, 12 February 2014
I've hurt my back.
I've pulled a muscle.
It goes into spasm.
Then I giggle.
That makes it worse.
So, I giggle more.
Anyway, I was walking to the car in SuperValu when I took a spasm.

And giggled.
And spasmed.
And giggled harder.
And spasmed.
So anyway, if any if you saw me apparently breakdancing across SuperValu car park I apologise.
It was a medical emergency.
My dancing isn't usually that good.

Tuesday, 25 February 2014
Its dissident weight watcher's night.
I went out for a walk.
Two of the bouncers at the door saw me.
They smiled at me.
To the casual observer, it would appear to be an encouraging smile.
I know different.
It's a knowing smile.
They are saying we have you.
They are saying you don't know it yet.
They are saying we admire your spirit.
They are saying we are going to break you into teeny skinny pieces.
They are saying we will charge you a fiver a week for the humiliation.
They stand there and smile knowingly.

But they don't have me.
They don't have me yet.
I'm going to order a dominos.
And a Chinese.
And an Indian.
And a Chippy.
And get it delivered to the dissident weight watchers.
And I'm going to stand at the end if the lane.
And watch the panic.
And smile knowingly back at them.

Monday, 3 March 2014.
Today is the Hells Bells birthday.
Today is also our anniversary.
A few years ago on the Hells Bells 18th birthday there was a band called Deja Vu playing in the Northgate.
I paid her in for her birthday.
2 pounds it was.

2 pounds sterling.
The Hells Bells stuck the lips on me.
I was looking good to be fair, with my Billy Ray Cyrus haircut, newly broken nose
and missing front tooth.
And she is still sticking the lips on me today.
Best 2 quid I ever spent.
So, Happy Birthday Hells Bells.
And Happy Anniversary.
And you still owe me 2 quid. xx.

Tuesday, 4 March 2014
I've made a social faux pas.
I've just been informed that stonemasons from Cullyhanna and Crossmaglen built
the Sistine Chapel.
Michelangelo was just the painter.
He stuck a couple of coats of emulsion on top of the lovely cut stone.
He then took all the credit.
Don't mention his name in South Armagh, it still rankles with them.
As I have just found out.

Thursday, 6 March 2014
I went to Bells for the paper.
There was a man in front of me in the queue.
He was unshaven.
He was wearing a long black coat and an army camouflage cap.
You know the type.
I ordered a magazine he said to the server.
Did it come he asked?
My curiosity piqued.
What type of magazine I wondered?
Top shelf brown paper bag quiet night in alone type of magazine?
One that had to be ordered separately?
Jaysus, what sort of character is this?
I took a step back and bumped the lady behind in the queue.
Sorry mouthed me. I didn't want to draw attention to myself.
What's the name the shop worker asked.
God help her the poor innocent child.
He told her his name.
And the name of the magazine she asked.
He leaned in and whispered.
I leaned in too but it was on my deaf side so I didn't hear.
The server went off to look.

We waited.
He nodded apologetically for the delay.
I nodded back because he was scary and obviously into some dodgy mags.
I nodded at the woman behind.
She covered here name badge with her hand.
Here we go the shop worker says.
She held it up.
She waved it around.
I couldn't look.
But i couldn't look away.
Star Wars comic she said.
Issue 6 she said.
He smiled with happiness.
I smiled with relief.
The lady in the queue reached for her pepper spray.
The shop worker then called next, the spell was broken and life went on.

Tuesday, 11 March 2014
Today's musings are about possessions.
I enjoy some of the finer things in life. I like a nice wine or whiskey. I enjoy a nice
cheese. I have a nice car. I live in a nice house. I have a boat, I play golf, I have a
wee jet ski and the effin bike.
But the best days I have had on the boat are with family and friends and falling in
and pushing in. The best nights in the house are when its full and bright and noisy.
The best golf days never happen alone, it's the craic and the slobbering and the
cheering and jeering and the pint afterwards that makes it. I enjoy the various
discussions about the effin bike (its doing well thanks for asking) just as much if
not more than actually using it. I enjoy wine and cheese but I would prefer a greasy
Chinese and a Beer with the gang.
I think we should all be proud of our various possessions. For me the real joy
comes from sharing with friends and family. I don't know where all that came
from. Barney says share and all that shite. But Barney might have had a point.

Tuesday, 11 March 2014
I'm cursed with an overactive imagination and an underactive thyroid.

Friday, 14 March 2014
I walked into the living room to the Hells Bells.
The bikes knackered says me.
Oh, she says with a wee hopeful smile.

Yeah says me. chain rusted and caught in the gears which caught in the wheel and pulled them right around and bent and twisted them and now they are banjaxed says me.

What are you going to do now she says with a big smile?

Scrap it says me.

No point spending money on it says me.

Ok says she grinning like a Cheshire cat.

No more effin motorbike she says bouncing with joy.

Oh, not the motorbike says me.

The pushbike says me.

No, the motorbike is fine and dandy.

Silence.

Tuesday, 18 March 2014

You know the way yawns are contagious?

So is bra strap adjustment.

We were in a cafe when one lady adjusted her strap.

This strap was the size of a seatbelt and almost the same colour.

There was an audible groan as the fibres took the strain.

Within one minute every female on the cafe had adjusted the bra, moved things north, then closer together to say hello, then further apart so they could see their dinner through the gap.

Some of the younger ones had handsfree bras, they just gave a wiggle and a shuffle and all was set.

It's true.

Bra strap adjustment is contagious.

Friday, 4 April 2014

Anyway, there was a report on BBC news this morning about the struggle to find a mate for the giant panda in Edinburgh.

Giant Pandas are big.

They are very laid back.

Their heads have white hair, their bodies dark.

They have big sad eyes.

They mate once a year.

I sound like a perfect match.

I'm going to phone Edinburgh zoo and offer my services.

Monday, 7 April 2014

I had a meeting in the MandS cafe in Forestside.

They wanted a skinny decaf latte.
I wanted tea.
I went up to order.
One skinny decaf latte please says me.
The cashier immediately pushed a button on the till.
And a tea says me.
The cashier looked puzzled.
Tea says me.
With milk says me.
Hold on a second she says.
She turned to person making the skinny decaf latte.
Do we have a button for tea she asked?
They examined the till looking for a button for tea.
Sorry says she.
Its ok says me.
I finally got my tea.
It was nice.
So was the skinny decaf latte.
And apparently much more popular.

Thursday, 10 April 2014
I need a haircut.
I keep putting it off.
I don't like haircuts.
I used to be fine until I met a barber called JJ.
JJ once cut JLS hair but he was at pains to point out that he is not their actual stylist but likes to think of himself as their Belfast stylist. JJ moved home from London to Belfast to be closer to his mammy in Cookstown. JJ wouldn't go to Cookstown because it's too small for him sexually.
JJ examined my head.
There was a lot of humming and hahing and pushing my head left and prodding my head right.
JJ appeared stumped.
JJ appeared confused.
JJ suggested he should cut the top of my head a touch shorter.
JJ suggested he should leave the sides a wee bit longer.
JJ suggested that this would bring my ears into a more natural place.
I leaned my head left.
I leaned my head right.
I asked him what the feck was wrong with my ears.
I still don't know how my ears are not in a natural place.
I still don't know if its placement or alignment or angle or dangle or shape or wind deflection that's unnatural.

That's why I don't like haircuts.
It's possible JJ had something to do with JLS splitting up.
I wonder if it was anything to do with their ears.

Monday, 14 April 2014

I was in top road petrol station paying for the rashers and eggs when I got a call from a client saying he was at the house with cash for me.
Don't leave I roared.
I'm on my way I lied.
I'm just at the end of the lane I promised.
Be careful he says.
There some dodgy characters hang about there he says.
OK but todays a safe day says me.
There's a ceasefire today says me.
I paid for the rashers and eggs and ran out of the garage and leapt into the car and drove like an eejit back to the house to meet the client and get paid. After he left I went out to car to get the rashers and eggs only to find in my haste I had taken the shopping home still in the shopping basket.
If any of you hear of a robbery on top road where the dashing young outlaw with the sexy brogue managed to get away with a haul of a shopping basket, it was me.
Now I have to figure out how to return the basket. and not get caught.

Tuesday, 15 April 2014

25 years ago, I was studying for the leaving.
It was a Saturday.
I worked like a Trojan all morning to keep the afternoon free for the football.
It was FA cup semi-final day, Liverpool v Forest.
They were the two best teams in Europe at that time.
FA cup semi-final day then isn't like it is now.
Football just wasn't live as much on television, so the chance to see a big game was not to be missed.
Shortly after 3 it became clear something was drastically wrong.
Brucie screaming at the stadium staff.
He was pointing at the crush in the crowd.
He could see it.
We could see it.
Why the hell couldn't the Police see it?
He went running back to his net.
He was trying to get the referee.
People were getting lifted out to the upper tier.
It took ages and ages and ages to get one small gate opened.
There were bodies on the pitch.

People were giving mouth to mouth.

There were no ambulances.

Advertising hoardings had to be used as stretchers.

police assumed it was a riot and forming a line on the halfway line to stop the trouble instead of treating the dying.

This was all broadcast live to my mammy's living room.

I kept waiting for the credits to roll like it was a movie.

It wasn't a movie.

There have been casualties.

10 dead.

20 dead.

30 dead.

Two lads from school were at the game.

It shook me then.

It's shaking me now.

Then the lies started.

They lied about fans breaking gates.

They lied about ticket less fans.

They lied about drunk fans.

They lied about fans stealing from the dead.

They lied about fans urinating on the dead.

They let 96 people die, and then they lied about it.

Wednesday, 16 April 2014

I'm in funny form this week. I'm in funny form every week, but this week it's a maudlin kind of funny form rather than a giddy kind of funny form.

I was driving down the road when I met a big lad who always walks the road on his own. I vaguely know his face from the adult centre or gateway but not his name. I always beep and wave, because he is always on his own. And he always perks up and grins from ear to ear and waves and turns and watches me down the road still waving and smiling. It makes him happy, and it makes my day.

Today was different.

Today he saw me first.

He waved. He gave me a big cheery happy unashamed uncaring wave.

I was the one that perked up and grinned from ear to ear.

Cheers bud.

You made my day.

Saturday, 26 April 2014

I have been informed by a very lovely lady in a funny hat that the dissident weight watchers out the end of the lane is in fact a splinter group calling itself Slimming World. This lady claims that they come in peace, and they mean me no harm. I in

ny role as founder member and chairperson treasurer and chief objectioner in the
Lower down the lane beside Slimming World Residents Association' would like to
announce that as dialogue has commenced we will not be objecting to this week's
activities.
Who would have thought it?
Slimming World and me.
Working together towards a shared future.
Thank goodness they don't fly a Slimming World flag, or hostilities would
recommence.
I haven't gone away you know.

Sunday, 27 April 2014

I'm out for a stroll along the Lagan towpath. There are certain social niceties to be
observed when strolling. I am an amateur walker. I am allowed to speak to other
amateur walkers. I can say morning. I can say grand morning isn't it.
On no account am I allowed to speak to professional walkers who pump arms. I
also have to avoid racing cyclists, they will only swerve around me to save damage
to their bikes. Mountain bikers will actively try to hurt me.
Mountain bikers like to yell watch out at us walkers from right behind us. It's fun
to yell something just as they pass by, then stand peering at the other side of the
river. They don't get the sarcasm.
I stopped in the Lock Keepers Inn. Those with a wry sense of humour and a
passing interest in local politics may share my amusement at the staff uniforms.
The logo on the back reads #lovethelockkeepers.
It is not advisable to take this literally.
The cyclists don't get the irony.
The mountain bikers and politicians are contemplating taking advantage of the
offer.

Friday, 2 May 2014.

I'm at the doctors.
I've heard all the rumours about man flu.
I've heard men are terrible patients.
I've heard men are always sick.
So why is the waiting room full of women?

Wednesday, 7 May 2014

I took a sales call from Bavarian Mini on Boucher Road.
I thought she said from Bavarian Massey on Boucher Road.
I had visions of rows of gleaming Massey Fergusons lined up beside the Ferrari
garage.

I could see queues of farmers in their Isuzu troopers with broken back lights on the sheep trailers coming up the M1.
I could smell the lines of slurry all the way from Cullybackey and Ccoalisland up through the West link.
I had a vision of salesmen in suits running in and out of Agnews trying to get the sheep back in the trailer.

The it became clear that they do Minis. If you want a Massey you will have to go elsewhere. I was disappointed.

Wednesday, 21 May 2014
I was given a nice wee gadget.
I was given a keyring that beeps and flashes when you whistle so that you won't lose your keys.
There is however one tiny problem.
I am by nature mostly a happy chirpy chap.
I whistle a lot every day.
Every time I whistle my keys beep and flash.
I have explained to the beeper and flasher keyring that this is recreational whistling not work related whistling but the beeper and flasher keyring does not see the difference.
I had to take the difficult decision to either stop whistling or make the beeper flasher redundant.
There is no whistler anonymous meetings or whistle watchers group locally, therefore I have decided to forcibly retire the beeper and flasher.

Has anyone seen my keys?

Tuesday, 3 June 2014
I'm going for a walk.
It's weigh in night at slimming world up the hill. It's packed.
Its pay in night at the funny church across the road. Its packed too.
Its band night in the orange hall down the hill. Its packed too.
I'm going to go for it.
Sometimes you just have to live on the edge.

Friday, 6 June 2014
What do you want to do Sunday says me?
Kids are away all day says me.
Don't know she says.
Spin up the coast says me?

Aye she says.
Walk up the forest park says me?
Sounds good she says.
Mosey on to Bushmills for a pub lunch and a wee snifter says me?
Now you are talking she says.
And then to wander to Portstewart for an ice-cream says me?
That sounds like a perfect day she says.
On the effin bike says me?

Silence.

Friday, 4 July 2014
My two women are away for the weekend.
No men allowed or wanted they gleefully informed me.
Girlie weekend they squealed.
They folded up the tea towels.
They straightened the display towels that aren't used.
They dusted the curtains that aren't for pulling.
They checked all the toilet seats were down.
They packed up the hairspray and the straighteners.
They brought their wine, their Wkds and their Alpen lights.
No men this weekend they cheered.
No world cup.
No golf.
EastEnders and chick flicks.
Woo hoo.
Their lift came.
Three more ladies.
More woo hooing.
The fake tan and perfume was making my eyes water.
No men for the weekend they confirmed.
They squeezed all 15 cases into the boot.
They disappeared down the lane to the sound of 'Sisters are doing it for themselves'

Twenty mins later on the M2 at Antrim they got a puncture. Guess who they phoned......

Monday, 7 July 2014
I went to top road garage.
I bought spuds and sausages and other bits.
I bought a carrot and parsnip pot for one.

It was 79p special offer.
The wee lady serving me lifted it up.
She turned it over.
Carrot and parsnip for one was on the bottom.
Microwave on only 2 and a half minutes.
She looked at me.
She gave me a wee sad knowing smile.
I wanted to say that I was having dinner with the family.
I wanted to explain that the kids don't like carrot and parsnip and that the wee pot is perfectly fine for me and the Hells Bells.
I wanted to tell her that we would all eat together and chat for an hour then Dave would make a cuppa and Emma would locate some fig rolls from somewhere while wife and I put our four feet up and that we would all yarn about our day and laugh and tease each other.
But i didn't.
I smiled back sadly.
I left.
With my carrot and parsnip for one.

Tuesday, 29 July 2014
Big brother Tommy called me.
Do you fancy a spin to Bray he says?
Aye says me.
In August, he says.
Aye says me.
For charity, he says
Aye says me.
Aine is going he says.
Aye says me.
On a bike, he says.
I should have said no.
I should have said not a hope.
I should have said it's not going to happen.
I said aye.

So, I had to go to Chain Reaction to buy a bike.
What about this one the assistant says.
It's only 8 kilos he says.
No way, really says me?
I weighed mine this morning says me.
I used the luggage scales says me.
We are just back from holidays says me.
Portugal says me.

It was lovely says me.
I was babbling because I had no idea whether the bike I was examining in detail was for boys or girls, and there certainly didn't seem to be any stabilisers or a basket for it.
Did you do any cycling out there he says.
Feck no, are you mad says me?
My bike is 15 kilos says me.
15 he repeated incredulously.
Aye 15 says me.
I didn't know they made road bikes that heavy he says.
Oh aye says me, they go all the way to 20.

All was going well until he suggested a fitting.
Just hop up on the turbo trainer he says.
A gang of assistants appeared from nowhere to watch and assist the assistant. Up I clambered.
Did you ever see lads in France flying on the bikes with their knees tucked in?
As I plopped onto the saddle the seat gripped the sides of my arse and forcibly shoved acres of skin back up me anus. This resulted in a huge tug on me genitalia which surrendered quickly. This pulled on my inner thighs which tucked my knees in tight. The assistant was very impressed at my cycling stance with the knees tucked in. I was more worried about my nether regions and whether the square yards if skin would ever reappear?
I feel as if I'm reaching says me.
Aye you have wee stumpy arms he says.
The assistants' assistants came over to look at the freak on the bike with the knees tucked in and the wee stumpy arms.
They agreed about the arms.
I paid a deposit. 50 quid. I agreed to pay it just to get off the bike.
We will need a final fitting upon collection he says.
I may or may not go back.
It depends on the genitalia.

Friday, 1 August 2014
I'm in Tuam in Co Galway. The ladies are going shopping and I don't have the ability or the aptitude to shop. I decided to go for a stroll. There was a Garda car outside a shop with a wee teenage ginger guard driving. He had nice eyes, so I stopped and asked for advice.
Hello Guard says me.
I'm here for an hour and looking for something to do says me.
Well you could try the cathedral he says, but I think it's closed today.
I see a sign for an old mill, what's that says me?
It's an old mill he says sadly, but it's closed too.

It's Market Day today he says, brightening.
There's a market at the square he says.
Is it a big market says me?
Tis surely, he says with enthusiasm, it's a grand big stall all right.

I went to the market. On the way, I passed the old mill. It was closed. There was a wee memorial garden for Anne McHugh from Tuam who died in the twin towers. Nice quiet place beside a stream. I found the cathedral, it was closed. The market had one stall. It was a grand big stall all right but still only one stall. I went to Eason's.

I was on the way back when a squad car pulled in beside me.
How did you get on says my wee ginger friend?
I hadn't realized that this was a homework assignment so I had a momentary panic.
I saw the old mill and the cathedral and the market says me.
I saw the memorial garden for Anne McHugh, God bless her and keep her says me.
The guard was pleased.
She was a cousin of mine he says.
Ahh sorry for your loss says me.
His partner leaned forward. His partner was swarthy and Mexican looking.
She was a cousin of mine too he said.
Ahh sorry for your loss too says me.
That was Tuam. I'm off to Craughwell. I can't stand the excitement here.

Saturday, 9 August 2014
I got a pump.
I pumped the new bikes tyres.
I got a drinks holder.
I put that on the new bike.
I got a bottle for the drinks holder.
I put that in the drinks holder on the new bike.
That's enough for the new bike for today.
I'm knackered.
I don't want to burn myself out.
Tomorrow I might try riding it.......

Tuesday, 12 August 2014
I park in a 9 level multi storey car park in Belfast every Tuesday.
Level 1 and 2 are full of the hard-working high earning people in posh cars with personalised plates, usually at their desks at 7am.

Level 3 and 4 are two types of people. You get the bigger posher cars with personalised plates that want a bit of room around so they park at the end spaces. You also the workers arriving for 8am fill in the rest.

Level 5 and 6 are the ones arriving at 9am. Their cars not as clean. They usually leave kids' stuff in the back. They show a better work life balance.

Level 7 and 8 is my territory. I wander in between 10am and 11am, breakfast remains in the car, golf clubs in the boot, teenage or young adult stuff in the back. The work life balance is skewed towards life.

Level 9 and 10 is like the isolation wing in prison. These levels house some of the most dangerous offenders and the traffic wardens. You don't want to be up there.

Anyway, today I got a space on level 1. I squeezed in between an Audi A3 with a personalised plate and a Mini Cooper with a personalised plate. It was a rare treat. The anti-slip on the floor was luxurious. The lights were slightly dimmer, creating a sensual but comforting ambience. The surrounding buildings sheltered me from the draught that can blow further up. All in all, it was a very pleasant place to park.

Next week I will back up to 8 where I belong. While the red-carpet treatment was nice for a day I did miss my mates. See you next week park buddies. If 8 is full I'm not going to 9. I will park at Abbey Centre and walk.

Monday, 18 August 2014
The Hells Bells is working from home today.
I'm going to have to try cut down on my whistling.
It's going to be tough.
I've just had everything my own way for so long.
She is now trying to work, and the whistling distracts her.
She hasn't said anything.
She just looks at me and sighs.
She sighs in disappointment.
This typing is now distracting her.
She just muttered.
I better stop now.
No whistling.
No typing.
I'm not sure I can cope with much more of this.
It's been 15 minutes of hell.

Thursday, 18 September 2014
I called in to the chippy on my way home from the golf.
Fish supper please.
I pulled a tenner from among the golf balls and tees in my pocket.

She went to hand me back in my change.
As I leaned over the counter to get it there was a clanking sound.
The lady looked at the change and the counter to see what she had dropped.
It wasn't you love says me.
It was me says me.
My balls just banged on the counter.

You should see the size of the fish she just served me. I think she likes me.

Friday, 19 September 2014
We have plans for the weekend.
We are heading to Galway for the East Galway Cancer Charity cycle followed by a catch up with the O Connor gang.
I've been in training all week.
These big events are all about preparation and planning.
You really don't want to go in for these things if you are not ready.
It's not fair on the other entrants.
I've been building up on the carbs and protein, especially pasta.
I've also been taking plenty of cheese and dairy products.
Vitamin B6 in a must.
Early nights all week to build up stamina.
Hot baths to ease muscles.
Stay off the fizzy juice all week.
Definitely no alcohol or caffeine.
I have planned ahead.
I know my limits.
I'm going to try to get as close to the max as i can without failing.
I have milk for beforehand.
I have snacks for during.
Vitamin c and a banana for afterwards.
I have bottles of water to take at the end of the night.
I have Rennie for the next morning and a wide range of pills.
Stretching exercises for both arms and the jaw muscles.
Holding in my wee to stretch the bladder.
You need to be ready for a night with the O Connors.

I prepared for the cycle too.
I adjusted the strap on the funny hat thing.
I squeezed the tyres to make sure they had some air.

Tuesday, 30 September 2014
I was walking down the stairs of the multi storey car park level 9.

was whistling away.
A Robbie Williams song.
Candy.
A lad came out of level 7.
He was also whistling.
He was whistling to the proclaimers.
I would walk 500 miles.
He was a good whistler.
I'm a reasonably competent whistler, but he was good.
I decided to join in.
I hoped he wasn't a sensitive whistler.
I hoped he would react badly.
I hoped he wouldn't view my whistling as heckling.
He whistled his badabumbum.
I did a badabumbum.
He approved.
We both did the badabumbumbumbumbumbumbumbum.
We reached level 1.
He nodded to me. I nodded back.
We went our separate ways.
Still whistling.

Thursday, 30 October 2014
I went to the Petrol station in Monkstown for a sausage baguette.
You want butter she says?
Please says me.
She butters the baguette.
You want sauce she says?
Ketchup please says me.
She put the ketchup on the baguette, but before the sausages were in it.
I was stunned.
She acted as if this was normal behaviour.
They just do things differently in Monkstown i suppose.
Now I have to try and eat a sausage baguette upside-down.

Sunday, 2 November 2014
Can I discuss Christmas lights and plastic Santa's and inflatable reindeer and that sort of stuff outside a house?
Can I tell you a wee story?
I used to think they were tacky and unnecessary.
I used to cringe looking at the state of some of the houses.
I never did anything like that on my house.

However, a few years ago, when the kids were small, there was a house nearby with loads of stuff.

This house was at a layby on the way out of Carrick.

The kids called it Santa's house.

Every time we went out in the car they wanted to go past Santa's house.

Santa's house Daddy please!!

Santa's house Mummy please!!

We groaned and moaned.

The kids loved it, so we always begrudgingly went.

We all oohed and aahed at the sea of plastic and lights from the safety of the layby.

One time the kids and myself had stopped outside in the layby and we were looking at all the lights.

A wee pensioner came out of the house.

He invited us in to see the lights inside.

We have loads he says.

We have the inside all decorated he says.

I immediately declined.

The kids immediately cheered.

Decision made, so in we went.

His wife greeted us like long lost friends.

Inside they had the biggest tree I've ever seen.

There were more plastic snowmen, complete with Santa and lights and presents.

They had multi coloured homemade paper chains from corner to corner, meeting at the centre light.

There were socks hanging on the mantelpiece.

They offered us a drink.

I immediately declined.

The kids immediately cheered.

I will have to have a word with those children about all this cheering.

They gave us the weakest diluted orange I have ever tasted, served in a very flimsy paper party cup.

Do you do it for the grandkids I asked.

No came the reply.

They looked at each other.

We do it for our daughter.

She was profoundly disabled.

She passed 5 years ago.

She loved Christmas and the lights.

We do it in her memory.

It's silly really.

No, it's not silly. It's anything but silly.

I felt like a condescending schmuck.

These people were doing one of the most wonderful beautiful things I have ever heard of, and I was standing here sneering at their efforts.

The wee house at the layby is now empty. It has been for a few years.

Friday, 14 November 2014

I was taking wee daughter to school on her non-uniform day.

Are ye up says me.

I'm getting up now says wee daughter.

No rush says wee daughter.

Its non-uniform day today says wee daughter.

It will only take me 5 minutes to get ready says wee daughter.

I don't have much experience with females. My mammy is one. So is my sister. And indeed, my wife. I have seen others from a distance. I have spoken to one or two. They seem nice enough people. But even i know that when a female has to choose her outfit on a non-uniform day there is not a hope in hell of it only taking 5 minutes to get ready.

Are ye up now pet?

I'm getting up now Daddy....

Tuesday, 2 December 2014

I'm in the bad books.

It's my own fault.

Nice earrings love says me.

Thanks, she says.

When did you get them says me?

While you were away with your brother she says she.

Oh, when I was away cycling on Saturday says me?

No when you were away climbing Slieve Gillion in June says she, but I'm glad you finally noticed......

Thursday, 11 December 2014

I have to be on the road today so I went into the mace to get a cup of tea to take with me. The local mace lets you make your own tea, and I'm choosy about my tea. But now unfortunately they make it behind the counter for you, and I don't like that. I walked to the deli counter.

What can I get you love the server says.

Tea please says me.

OK darling milk and sugar she says?

Just milk says me.
She put the milk in first.
I was gutted.
It's never the same with the milk in first.
The lady was lovely so i resolved not to let my disappointment show.
There you go pet she says.
Thanks, i grunted.

I went to the till.
I was fighting back tears.
The lady at the till scanned the tea, and then scanned my packet of Exy Ozys beef flavour snack pack for 30p.
As she put the Exy Ozys back on the counter she nudged the tea and sent it splashing all over my left foot.
Now i had a burning left foot and wet sock to go with my already fragile emotions.
Oh, my goodness, I'm sorry she says.
I will get you another one she says.
Come on she says.
Sorry she says.
We went back down to the deli counter to make me another tea.
Milk and sugar she says?
Just milk says me.
She made the tea and then put the milk in last.
I smiled.
She smiled.
The deli lady smiled.
I squelched away with my burning left foot and wet sock into the cold and wet outside.
I was happy.
I had the milk in last.

Monday, 29 December 2014
Would you like a glass of wine and some cheese love?
No thanks I'm grand.
Ok what about a glass of cider and some snacks?
No thanks I'm happy as I am.
What about a mug of tea and some chocolate digestives?
Now you are talking big lad.

Tea biscuits and Coronation Street in front of the gas fire. We are wild and we don't care.

Wednesday, 7 January 2015
A wee observation.
I like when people say God Bless at the end of a conversation.
I like that phrase.
Ok now Bye bye God Bless bye bbb bye.
Anyway, good luck. See you. God bless.

Friday, 9 January 2015
Would you be interested in a business proposal he says?
Give me the details says me.
So, he did.
It looked good.
The finances were good.
The exit strategy was good.
Financing and location and costings and return all looked spot on.
Then he poured the tea.
He put the milk in first.

It was looking so good for so long there.

Thats a shame.

Saturday, 10 January 2015
I'm watching Father Ted on RTE.
Mrs Doyle is making tea.
She put the milk in first.
I'm gutted.

Thursday, 15 January 2015
I was in Ballyhalbert recently.
There are signs on the way out saying 'Haste ye back'.
Isn't that a wonderful Ulster Scots expression.
Failte agus Slan Abhaile.
Aren't they wonderful Irish expressions.
I'm a fan of bluegrass.
Take the High Road.
Will ye go Lassie go.
Flower of Scotland.
And Irish folk.
And Irish country.

I like the idea of the reels and the jigs, but I can't tell the Scots versions from the Irish versions.
After 10 minutes of either I slope off looking for the disco.

Here is my point.
I enjoy Ulster Scots. I enjoy Irish.
I enjoy the expressions.
I enjoy the phrasing, the accents, the place names.
I have nothing to fear from either language, but a hell of a lot to gain from both.
It's a pity our wonderful political representatives can't put away their bitter inbred sectarian ways for 10 seconds to stop their point scoring.
Promote both languages and traditions and beliefs and superstitions.
Tell people that we have nothing to fear.

Anyway, haste ye back. I'm aa daen. Eneuch. Maith thu. Oiche maith.
I'm off to the Broadisland Gatherin.
I'm looking for the disco.

Saturday, 24 January 2015
I was making tea and toast earlier.
I have a nice block of Red Leicester cheese.
As I started to cut the cheese I thought about Granny Murphy.

Many years ago, when i was a wee lad I was cutting some cheese. I was trying to cut a full rectangular slice sideways across the full block of the cheese. Granny Murphy told me I was doing it wrong. Granny Murphy was a proper granny, not like the Grannys you get nowadays. Grannys nowadays are more like yummy mummies than Grannys. Granny Murphy always had soup in the pot and tea on the boil, and sugar sandwiches, and hair in a bun and always in an apron. These are the things a proper grannys should have.

Anyway, Granny Murphy took the knife and cut a wee triangle from the left corner of the cheese to the middle of the short side. She did the same from the middle of the short side to the right corner. This left the cheese in a house shape. She gave me one piece to eat, and she ate the other. Then she cut the cheese left right left right at a slight angle from the side to the middle in perfect wee slices, making the house shape a wee bit shorter every time. When I cut cheese nowadays I make a wee house shape and I eat the corners. And then I cut my wee slices. And I smile at the memory of Granny Murphy.

Saturday, 31 January 2015

. was in the Mace in the queue with my sausage bap. There was a scrawny woman
n front of me, and in front of her was a little lad with a bottle of Lucozade
Sport 99p and a pound coin in his wee hand. A second till opened and scrawny
ook her opportunity to dive in front of wee lad and get served first. Scrawny then
finished and was leaving. The server said next please.
I say to wee lad go on ahead wee man, I will wait, I have manners.
Scrawny turned around and fixed me with a stare that would blanch the bollox of a
lesser man. I stared back.
I was quite proud of myself.
My mammy would have been proud of me.
I'm finally using the manners my mammy gave me.
That will make my mammy happy.

Then a roar came from behind me.
HOWL ANN SHUN. SCUZE ME. SCUZE ME.
It was the wee lads mummy, 4-foot-tall, bleach blond hair not combed in the recent
past, Ugg boots, a onesie with pink hearts on it carrying a basket full of pop tarts
and frozen pizza.
She got served.
She remembered the Coke.
Off she went in her Uggs and her onesie for the Coke.
I waited.
I have manners.
My mammy is proud.
The onesie and Uggs eventually came back.
She eventually found her purse.
She eventually paid.
She eventually put her change back in the purse.
She eventually waddled away, pink hearted onesie straining at the seams.
By this stage scrawny is probably at her desk with an hour's work done.
I'm still standing in the mace with a sausage bap gone cold.
I've still got my principles.
I've still got my manners.
My mammy is still proud.

Manners are sometimes overrated mammy.

Friday, 13 February 2015
I've hidden the ropes off the trailer.
I've hidden the ping pong bats.
I've hidden the ping pong balls.
I've locked away the jump leads and the battery booster pack.
I've gotten rid of the gaffa tape, insulating tape and selotape.

I lost the shovel, the spade, the rake, and definitely the garden fork.
I've taken the plug off the strimmer and the hedge clippers.
I misplaced the dogs lead and collar.
I got rid of the rulers in the house.
I cut all the cable ties in half.
I hid my spare golf club stash.
I got rid of all the belts in the house.

You can't be too careful when the women are out to see 50 shades.......

Friday, 27 March 2015

I've been watching the Clarkson furore, and wondering whether we should admire him for his abilities or admonish him for his failings.
It made me think about a man with limited abilities and massive weaknesses. He is a man I genuinely admire, for overcoming hurdles and making the most of what he has.

This man isn't famous.
He has a face like a cement mixer that has been hit too many times with a shovel.
He has a limp and a lisp.
He can't quite pronounce his own name.
He has a wee job, and he does to the best of his abilities.
He always goes that extra mile.
He always helps in little ways.
This man used to be an alcoholic.
He lived on the streets for almost 10 years.
On the streets to him meant sometimes a hostel, sometimes a shelter, sometimes a bus station.
He had a daughter.
And he had a suit.
He always found somewhere to store the suit and he always remembered where it was.
The daughter and the suit were his last connections with normal life.
Once or twice a year he would find somewhere to shower and shave.
He would go visit his daughter.
He would tell her how well he was doing.
He would sit there gaunt and failed and weathered in a musty old suit and lie about how he was sober and working.
He would go back to drinking.

One time many years ago now he went to see the daughter.
He got the suit on.
He walked because he didn't have 50p for the bus.

He was welcomed in and shown to the good room.
He was told his daughter had passed away.
While he was lying to her about being sober, she was lying to him about her health.
He was told that they tried to find him at his address, his job, everywhere but that they couldn't find him for the funeral.
No one knew where he was.
He got a lift to the graveyard.
He said his goodbyes to his daughter.
He got a lift to Cuan Mhuire in Newry.
He got dry.
He stayed dry.
He got a flat.
He got a wee job.
There was where i was privileged enough to meet him and get his life story piece by piece over cups of tea in a wee security hut over a couple of years.

Last time I saw him he had bought a cheap wee runabout, and it meant the world to him. And we sat in his wee car and we had a wee cuppa.
He is still dry.
He still has the suit.
To me he is worth my admiration.
Every word of this is true.

Tuesday, 31 March 2015
Do you ever get a little twist of fate that gives you a wee boost when you are drifting toward the end of a cold wet Tuesday?
A tiny beam of sunshine in an otherwise drab and dreary day?
I had one of those today.
I was in Abbeycentre. I was in Texas or Homecare or whatever it's called this year.
I was looking for radiator valves.
They didn't have any.
As I was leaving a saw a wee something familiar glistening.
A wee thing that brought to mind me mammy and me Daddy and Mullens chips (after the movie why not treat yourself to a meal at Mullens, its clean healthy and wholesome) and Culletons shop and Fat Frogs ice lolly's and Marathons and 6 packs of Alien Spacers and a can of Fanta for a quid and Massey Fergusons and laughing at Davy Browns and drawing hay and Sprich bikes and Karl Lewis haircuts from the man opposite Boyds and much more besides.

This came about because the snack dispenser in Abbeycentre Texas or Homecare or whatever it's called this year is stocking southern Tayto cheese and onion.
It brought me back memories.
And that was enough to make my day.

Sunday, 5 April 2015
I put The Hells Bells and her buddy Elsie in the front of the boat at 45mph and told them that the wind in their faces will stretch their skin and give them a face lift. They give me that look and asked if I'm trying to say they need a facelift. I assured them they are grand but that it wouldn't do any harm.

And somehow, I'm the one in trouble?

Thursday, 9 April 2015
Yesterday was day 1 of my new fitness regime.
I limited myself to 1 pint last night and walked home from the Indian.
I'm proud of myself.

Friday, 10 April 2015
Another hero has fallen.
Bruce took a bribe.
Tiger got a beating off his missus.
Lance got caught stoned.
But the biggest of all is that now Adam Richman (Man v Food) has turned vegan.

Sunday, 10 May 2015
Pete and myself left Belfast early yesterday driving to Dublin to get the train to join the Cycle Against Suicide in Tullamore to cycle back to Mullingar then Dublin. We parked in donnybrook and hopped on the bikes to Heuston station to get the train to Tullamore. I thought it was a 25-minute cycle and we had an hour to do it. The timing was perfect.
Except it wasn't. I got a puncture, and it became a 60-minute cycle. A young lady with pink hair came off her barge on the canal to tell me I was grumpy but Pete was nice. She was half right. We got the bike fixed, and blasted down to Heuston on the wrong side of the road. We jumped red lights, flew past Kilmainham, skipped on to the footpath, tore flat out down to Heuston, ran across the carriageway, and cycled right into the station with minutes to spare sweating like eejits and giggling like schoolkids.
NO CYCLING ON THE PLATFORM yelled at us.
I got off the bike with my usual lack of poise because I can't lift my leg high enough to get over the saddle. I drop the bike. I step off the bike. I lift up the bike. We made the train.
We arrived in Tullamore. We went to the gate with Aine to greet the riders in. There were lots and lots of familiar faces. We were knackered clapping and only

half of them were in. We had tea and sandwiches. We had a powerful spellbinding speech from Joe Dixon. We had a headscratchingly brilliant and funny and sad speech from Jim Breen.

A song to finish. The Cycle Against Suicide song.
Everybody silent.
No one leaving.
No one moving.
No one coughing.
We sat in the sun with numb bums on the tarmac of Tullamore harriers.

We left Tullamore on the bikes. We eschewed the straight short road to Mullingar, we were touring the country. We flashed through Clara Moate Kilbeggan and Tyrellspass. A little lady in her first communion dress and her family all came out to wave us past. I ended up talking to a lady on the bikes. We talked crap for 20 minutes or so.
I asked why she was doing it.
She told me about her mid-50-year-old brother who had taken his own life in August, leaving 4 kids and devastating their 76-year-old mum.
She asked me why.
I started to tell her why I was doing it fitness, enjoyment, friendship, in memory of someone, to possibly help others.
She said no.
She said that's not what i meant.
She said I meant why did my brother do it?

I don't know pet.
I wish I did but i don't.

We talked some more, then we fist pumped which is the cycling equivalent of a squeezyhug.

We got to Mullingar. There was orange absolutely everywhere. The Street was packed with people cheering and clapping. There were drinkers and shoppers and smokers waving and clapping and cheering and high fiving. We got a welcome from the Mayor, and went out to Loreto for soup and sandwiches. We eventually made it out to the b&b to change and back to Mullingar to selfie crash a hen party, adorn a Joe Dolan statue with an effin bike t shirt, hug a huge wee bouncer before a cowboy supper and a taxi home from a local self-appointed counsellor.
Women talk he says.
Men don't.
I like to listen he says.
When the Lord above made time says me.
He made plenty of it he finished.

We called it a night.
Pete didn't make a move.
I had him warned.
I'm not putting out says me.
Not on the first date says me.
I'm not that kind of boy says me.

I still don't know the answer to why. i never will. But if that 55-year-old man with 4 kids and a devastated 76-year-old mum had seen the welcome in Mullingar, He would never ever have done it.

#itsoknottobeok. It's absolutely ok to ask for help.
Mullingar to Dublin today. Take care lads.

Saturday, 23 May 2015
There is a sign newly appeared on the hills above Belfast.
Remember Ballymurphy and Springhill 1971 1972.
I agree.
We should remember.
We should also remember Greysteel.
We should also remember Omagh.
We should also remember Enniskillen.
We should also remember Bloody Sunday.
We should also remember the Shankill Road.
We should also remember Loughinisland.
We should also remember every time somebody was murdered in this dirty wee sectarian war.
We should forget the bigotry.
We should forget the hatred.
We should move on from those.
We should remember the victims and do everything we can to never let it happen again.

Sunday, 24 May 2015
You know the way they have legalised gay marriage?
Is straight marriage still legal?
Or if i get married again do i have to marry a man?
Should i be on the lookout just in case?
Should I be evaluating potential partners?

He would have to play golf, like water sports and curry and ride a motorbike.
GSOH and all that. If interested please send picture (of motorbike).

Wednesday, 27 May 2015

There was a funny wee moment recently.

. was talking to a mate that happened to be at a do where one of the couples happened to be a same sex couple.

It wasn't commented upon.
It wasn't explained.
It wasn't treated as anything out of the ordinary.
It wasn't unusual.
It was just an ordinary day having an ordinary meal with an ordinary group.

Then he told me about the food.
There was a lasagne.
There was a chicken curry.
Then a look of disapproving disdain came on his face.
There was a vegetarian chilli he says.
For the veggies, he says scornfully.

So anyway, it appears that the gay community has reached a level of acceptance.
But the vegetarians?
Not sure about them lot apparently.

Sunday, 7 June 2015

I've just finished the Croi cycle, 75 miles around Lough Corrib in Galway.
I'm wearing my bib shorts. For the non-cycling muggles among you bib shorts have a strap that comes up over the shoulders. After the cycle I decided to take off the straps and let them hang for comfort. I didn't want to take of the cycling t shirt because I had just cycled 75 miles to get it, and there are lots of people about, and I suffer from crippling shyness.
You would think that this would be easy. Women do it all the time. They take the bra off through the sleeve, wave it round the head, and ping it across the room.
Actually, it's not easy.
I couldn't figure it out.
I think I needed to bring my arm out through sleeve.
I couldn't manage that.
I'm currently still wearing the bib shorts. and the strap is cutting me.

Respect to the women. try it if you don't believe me.

Thursday, 25 June 2015

I walked out of an upstairs office at 1pm going for the lunch. There was a blond lady coming down the stairs from above. I dandered on down, she followed. I came to the door to the street. I opened it and walked out, but paused to hold it open for the blond lady.

I turned right.

She turned right behind me.

She then took off down the footpath at pace.

I dandered with my usual lack of urgency. I'm made for stamina, not speed.

She passed me on the footpath and walked up to where a man was waiting on the corner.

Hello he says.

Stop you looking at my chest she says. (Larne accent)

I wasnae he says. (also Larne accent)

You was she says.

I could see ya she says.

You never took your eyes off it she says.

At this point I had heard the conversation as I was just dandering past. I really wanted to glance sideways and take a look but obviously I couldn't in case I got caught.

I just don't know how mesmerising the chest was. and not knowing is terrible. Next week I need to be there before 1pm, just to put my rampant imagination to rest.

Sunday, 5 July 2015

Pops and myself drove to Killarney for the Ring of Kerry charity cycle. We chatted and listened to LMFM radio the whole way down past Dublin, along the M50 and down the M8. It's a grand station with a bit of country and mainstream pop, the deaths and the adverts.

We passed Kildare and lost the LMFM. Excuse my naivety, but I just hit the up arrow for the next radio station. They are a strange lot in that neck of the woods. It's beyond the pale. It's a normal Friday morning and the radio people are talking about women's sexual health. I quickly changed the channel.

Jaysus lads me Daddy is in the car like!!

The next station was talking about pet names for your todger. Thor was suggested. And Spartacus. But the favourite in the area was apparently Russell the Muscle!! Pops found thus very amusing.

Finally, a song, all the single ladies. My daddy knew the tune. he hummed along. I know a bit of the dance. I was tempted to show him. He could then teach the lads at the active retirement. It was just a pity i had to drive. He hummed. I sang away to myself. Woh oh ooooooo woh oh ooooooo as we passed Portarlington on the M8.

Good times.

will bring a CD next time.
Or I will choose my radio station more wisely.

Monday, 6 July 2015
I did an upgrade on the Samsung.
It changed the colour on the messages page to orange. I can live with that.
It changed the diary function too. It has put in extra entries. This Sunday for example I now have an entry for Battle of the Boyne. On Monday I have an entry for Battle of the Boyne remembered. I never had those before.
I can only conclude that the Samsung update has turned my phone Protestant. I better watch my language. And keep my phone off the Falls Road.

Friday, 10 July 2015
Last week I did the 120-mile Ring of Kerry charity cycle.
We made Waterville, which was around 50 miles in.
I needed to pee.
I walked into the loo in a pub.
It was a big long stainless steel urinal.
It was full of cyclists.
I waited in the queue.
I spotted a gap so over I went.
I reached into my shorts to pee but I couldn't find it.
I checked left.
I checked right.
I checked front and back.
I had it that morning in the shower.
I distinctly remember tucking it into my shorts at the b&b.
Now it wasn't there.
I was worried that perhaps it was numb and I was actually holding it but couldn't feel it.
I swapped hands to check with my other hand.
I didn't put both hands into the shorts at the same time, that would have been weird.
I did it casually and discretely.
I couldn't find it with my either hand.
I crouched slightly while leaning left and backwards to check the reflection of my crotch in the stainless-steel urinal.
It wasn't polished enough to see a reflection.
I turned to my neighbour.
Excuse me says me.
He turned towards me.
He had his cycling shorts around his knees and his big blue eyes were full of tears.

Never mind says me.
I stepped away form the urinal.
I waited for a cubicle where I could wee like a lady.

It came back on Tuesday. I just reached in and there it was. Phew.

Friday, 24 July 2015
I bumped into a friend in Tesco.
How's the Hells Bells he says?
Grand says me.
The kids he says?
Grand too says me.
The effin bike he says?
Creaking and groaning but grand too says me.
And the….
The you know…..
He nodded…..
He raised his eyebrows and nodded twice…..
The auld you know…..
I was puzzled.
He looked left.
He looked right.
He leaned in.
I leaned in.
The auld penis he says.
How's the penis he says.
Did it every reappear after the cycle?

Carrick Tesco, Friday morning, a man asking after your penis.
The Hells Bells is right. Somethings should be private.

Saturday, 15 August 2015
A couple of years ago i was driving through Monaghan town with the boat on the
back. I was heading out the Aughnacloy road. I pulled in to the Emo petrol station
on the left for a snack. I went over to the ironically named deli counter. The server
came in from fiddling with a diesel pump, and I don't think she changed gloves.

I got served and paid and went outside to force down the sweet chilli chicken
diesel sandwich. There was a wee lad and his dad looking at the boat.
The wee lad was amazed.
The wee lad had special needs.

That's the engine son.
WOW DAD!!
That's where the captain sits son.
WOW DAD!!
That's the car that tows the boat son.
WOW DAD!!.
Then I did something a wee bit silly.
I asked the wee lad would he like a spin in the boat.
WOW!!!! he said.
Off came the covers.
Down went the ladder.
In went the wee lad.
In went dad.
Up went ladder.
Wee lad sat in the captain's seat.
Off we went.
Around the petrol station.
The diesel coated deli lady smiled and waved.
The lorry drivers rolled up their copies of the sun, put down their Yorkies and
waved.
The wee lad waved back.
We went around again.
Everyone waved and cheered.
The wee lad bounced and cheered back.
Around we went again.

Emo station, on the Monaghan to Aughnacloy road. I passed it last night. I thought
about a wee lad with special needs whose name I don't know who loves boats and
who made me do something silly and made me smile and who is still making me
smile today.

Friday, 4 September 2015
I was taking my wee daughter to school.
Daddy?
Yes pet.
Don't embarrass me like you did yesterday Daddy.
Ok pet.
Do you promise daddy?
I promise I won't embarrass you like i did yesterday pet.

I will most likely embarrass you in a whole new way pet.

Saturday, 19 September 2015

I'm gutted.

I'm devastated.

I just can't believe that my wife of 23 years and 8 days would betray me like that.

I know we have our ups and downs.

Every couple has.

Every road has its rocks.

Every Rose has its thorn.

But to be betrayed like this.

She was making tea.

I was making breakfast.

Rashers and eggs.

It was a scene of wedded bliss.

She didn't put the milk in first.

I checked.

Tea bag in.

Water in.

I gave a wee smile of approval, encouragement, pride.

I turned away to get the tea towel.

I turned back.

I caught the evil glint in her eye as she poured the milk into the tea.

WITH THE TEA BAG STILL IN THE CUP.

I yelled at her to stop.

She stopped.

She gave me the innocent look.

It was just the once she said.

It didn't mean anything she said.

It was just a silly mistake she said.

We are going to try and work through this.

We are going to try and be strong for the kids.

I will try to forgive her.

I will try to forget.

I will make my own feckin tea.

Saturday, 7 November 2015

I was having a chat with the Hells Bells

Its time I changed the effin bike says me.

Is it she says.

It is says me.

It's just tired says me.

Brakes are poor says me.
It's hard to start says me.
Its 29 years old says me.
It's too old for a daily rider says me.
OK says she.
OK? says me?
OK says she.
Just one thing says she.
When you change it could you change it to something with four wheels says she.
OK says me.
OK says she?
OK says me.

I am pretty sure the Hells Bells just told me to get two motorbikes.

Thursday, 12 November 2015
I'm unsettled.
I'm out of sorts.
I'm not myself.
My laptop became too old to be useful.
I've had it since 2004.
We have seen a lot together.
I find that laptops grow on you.
They are like pets, kids, part of the family.
I miss its sticky e and the way the battery would go from 60% to flat in 2 minutes.
My computer fried too.
It overheated and the case melted.
I got a new one but it's not the same.
It's fast and it's powerful but it's not the same.
My old one made all sorts of jet engine noises and whirrs and clunks and groans.
My new one is silent boring, efficient, judgemental.
My screen on the mobile phone broke.
I had to upgrade that too.
The Chinese takeaway has changed its curry sauce recipe.
Brekkie place doesn't do cheesy toasted sodas any more.
Everything has changed.
I don't like change.
Pay no heed.
I'm out of sorts.
I'm not myself.
I'm off to get some Tayto.
They haven't changed.

Saturday, 14 November 2015
I don't like pretentiousness.
I don't like gobshitery.
I'm in Abbey Centre shopping centre.
I'm out of my comfort zone here.
I can shop for books or trainers.
Anything else and I'm out of my comfort zone.
I wandered in to Costa coffee. There is no queue.
I ordered tea.
One man takes the order.
He tells another man who makes the tea.
The second man tells a girl on the till who charges you for your tea.
A second girl then motions you down past the till to collect your tea.
It's all very pretentious and gobshitery for one cup of tea.
Between the four of them no-one thought to ask if I wanted milk.
So, I stood there and waited.
Till girl noticed me and nodded to tea maker that I was still there.
Tea maker told order taker that I was still there.
Order taker came down the shop to see why I was still there.
I told him I would like some milk.
He told tea maker to get me milk.
I expected tea maker to go out the back and bring in a bullock whose job it was to get the cow.
Instead he simply poured milk into a jug and gave it to tray girl who was behind him.
Tray girl then squeezed past him to put the milk on the tray.
Anything else she says?
No thanks says me.
Believe it or not that's not the most pretentious thing about it all.
They put the saucer on the tray.
They put the tea spoon on the saucer.
They put the tea pot on the tray.
Then for some reason probably only known to Mr Costa currently playing up front for Chelsea I believe, they put the cup upside down balanced on top of the teapot.
I lifted the tray, while trying to hold my books and my trainers that I bought, and the cup slipped off its precarious position on the teapot and fell and broke.
Order taker appears to be quite upset with me.
Take a seat sir he snapped.
We will bring down a fresh cup he sneered.
With a spoon says me, queryingly.
With a spoon sir, he says.
So, I'm sitting typing a status while waiting for my cup and spoon.

don't need a spoon. I don't take sugar. I better not say anything. They appear to ꞓe quite irate with me.

really fancy a muffin. I better not.

Thursday, 26 November 2015
We have the painters in painting the living room. They put the first coat on. I came ꞓn at lunchtime, took one look at it and went that's horrible.
I know says the painter.
That's the colour your missus picked says the painter.
It's called Helium says the painter.
I still don't like it says me.
Me neither he replied.
Let's change it says me.
OK he says.
So, we changed it.

It was all good fun acting the big lad with the big painter making these decisions in Carrick while the Hells Bells was in Belfast.
But now I'm at home.
I'm alone.
I'm sitting in the living room.
The living room isn't Helium.
The Hells Bells is on her way home........

Monday, 30 November 2015
My wee baby daughter of only 17 walks in.
I got my first university offer today she says.
Fantastic says me.
It's only conditional but its an offer she says.
Still fantastic says me.
It's dependant on my grades she says.
Absolutely fantastic says me.
It's the course I really wanted she says.
Brilliant says me.
Thanks dad she says.
What university is it says me?
London, she says.

I waited for her to finish.
I wanted her to finish the London with derry.
I waited and waited.

She didn't say derry. She left it at London.
Crap.

Thursday, 3 December 2015
I drove out the lane carefully, because tonight is weigh in night.
Slimming World are on active service tonight.
As I went past I saw only one car at the Slimming World bunker.
I realised that Victory is mine.
For years now they have bullied, tortured and mentally brutalised me, to the point where the weighing night curry chip became inedible.
Three times a week they park in my lane and stare at me and block the exit and wear clothes that are see through but weigh very little.
Tonight however, attendances have dwindled until there is only one car.
But I am still standing.
I decided to celebrate.
I went for a chip.
Not just a chip, a salt and chilli double fried chip.
With onions and peas.
Deep fry the onions and peas please.
With curry sauce.
And full fat coke.
Coke with two sugars please.
I'm letting the hair down.
I'm pushing the boat out.
I'm celebrating.

I came back home.
I drove up the road.
The bunker was packed.
There was barely room to squeeze by.
They all looked at me.
The watched me with disdain.
The stared at me with disgust.
Several of them ogled me with desire.
I felt dirty.
They smelt the curry.
Maybe they sensed the curry.
I put my head down.
I went into the house.
I put the salt and chilli double fried curry chip with deep fried peas and onions in the bin.
I wouldn't have enjoyed it anyway.
I hate Slimming World.

Tuesday, 15 December 2015

took the effin bike into work Belfast, it was a dry day, with rain forecast at 4pm. I was riding along Oxford Street past the Law Courts when the pedestrian crossing lights went red, and I had to stop. Pastor McConnell was due in court today. Several of his supporters were on the footpath displaying their right to free speech by berating everyone else and drowning them out with a load speaker. I amused myself by revving the engine every time they raised the loudspaeaker to speak. It turns out that a Vtwin Honda with a hole in the exhaust is much louder than a ranting evangelical.

The lights went green.

had to go.

t was a pity. I could have stayed for hours.

left work at 3pm to get home before the rain.

The effin bike wouldn't start.

had to bump it.

had to push it as fast as I could along the footpath, jump on, into second, out with the clutch while dropping my arse onto the seat for maximum traction.

It took me three attempts before it started.

The pastor's mates would have wet themselves laughing.

Thursday, 17 December 2015

The Hells Bells was going for the 8am train to Dublin. She ran late. She had to ask me for a lift. I had to comply. She didn't want to. I didn't want to. But neither of us had a way out. It was too late for the taxi. I would have to do it. I'm built for stamina, not speed. I refuse to rush. This didn't bode well.

I went by the back road.

It's the way I always go.

It's quieter.

Its prettier.

Its longer.

Its slower.

She signed.

I went down Troopers lane.

I like when you go over the train tracks.

I slowed down.

I checked left and right along the tracks even though the barrier is up.

She harrumphed but changed it to a cough.

I turned onto Shore road.

It's a dual carriageway, but I only recognise the slow lane.

She tutted.

She tutted again at Greenisland.

She tutted at UUJ.
She tutted at the red lights at Jordanstown road.
She tutted at every gully and bump in between.
I decided to try the fast lane.
I indicated.
She looked at me in surprise.
I moved out.
She smiled approvingly.
I was quite enjoying it.
We passed a wee pensioner in the Micra that I had been following.
We passed quite a few cars.
I was tempted to move back in but I stayed out.
Then there was a van in front turning right.
I had to stop.
The wee Micra passed us back.
Another car and another passed us.
She tutted and tutted.
Every car that went past got a tut.
I thought my indicator was on.
Tut Tut Tut Tut Tut.
The van moved.
We got going.
I saw a gap in the slow lane.
I dived in.
I stayed there.
I was about 80 cars back from where I was originally but my nerves were shattered.
She made the train.
She was last to arrive.
She can try to tell the train driver to go on the other track, in the fast lane.
I don't care.
I'm going for a cuppa before the drive home. I need one.

Friday, 18 December 2015
I got worried when I was reading the Facebook.
Apparently, Isis and the Syrians are coming to get me.
Last year the gays were going to get me.
2 years ago, the Muslims were coming to get me.
5 years ago, the Bulgarians.
10 years ago, the Poles.
15 years ago, the Iraqis.
And the Irish.
And the British.

0 years ago, the Russians.
ll coming to get poor me.

don't think I need to worry about any of this lot, they won't get past Slimming
World at the end of the lane. I don't need Britain First or UKIP or the paramilitaries
r Willie Frazer to save me, I've got Slimming World on my side. If they get down
ne lane they would all have to climb over the homeless ex-servicemen and dodge
ne Syrian refugees that are apparently littered everywhere.

'm glad I'm so well informed. I'm glad of slimming world. For once.

Tuesday, 12 January 2016
Dear Hells Bells.
We need to talk.
made myself boiled eggs for breakfast.
went looking for egg cups.
couldn't find any.
found shots glasses 50ml.
found shots glasses 25ml.
The egg was too small for the big shot glasses.
t fell down inside it.
The egg was too big for the wee shot glass.
t perched to high on it and wasn't steady.
Then I found the spirit measure double sided thingy.
t was just right.
feel like goldilocks.
We need to get more egg cups. We need to do less shots.

Saturday, 23 January 2016
I'm sitting here with three women. Women are lovely people. I'm very fond of
them. My wife is one, my mammy is one, so is my sister, and indeed my daughter.
Women are also different to the rest of us normal people. I started thinking about
what I know about women. I know one thing they like, and one thing they dislike.

They dislike multi-function remote controls. They can't work them. They can multi
task but they can't multifunction. Check it out if you don't believe me. One remote
that works the TV and the Sky and the stereo is baffling to them.

Women love small change. I went to the Mace for a salad bowl with warm chicken
fillet and diet coke. £3.91. I pulled out the change. It was the ay after the night
before, and I had loads and loads of change. The trousers were barely clinging onto
arse cheeks. I hitched them up.

The girl looked at me interested.
I started counting.
50p pieces, 2 quid's worth.
I handed to the cashier.
Her cheeks were flushed.
20ps, brought us up to £3.40.
Her breathing had quickened.
10ps brought us up to £3.80.
She licked her lips.
I counted out the tuppences and a penny to finish.
She shuddered.
I stuck the rest in the charity jar.
She groaned.
I walked out, in a love them and leave them way.

That's all I know about women. The rest of it is a total feckin mystery.

Wednesday, 24 February 2016
I had a wee client come to see me.
I got a new van he says.
Did ya says me?
I did he says.
Can I see it says me?
Sure you can he says, all chuffed.
So out we went.
Very nice says me.
Very very nice says me.
Alloy wheels says me.
Very clean says me.
Nice registration number too says me.
And electric windows he says.
They go up and down themselves he says.
Do they says me.
They do he says.
Do you want to see he says?
I do says me.
He hopped in. He pressed the button. Nothing happened. He was sad.
Try it with the key in says me.
He did.
The window went down.
The window went back up.
The window went back down to make sure the first one wasn't a fluke.
The window went back up again.

hen he showed me the passenger window did the same.

wice.

just made my day.

made my day because I like people that value and enjoy and appreciate the little ings in life. I like people that get happy and excited over all they have, and don't et carried away about the things they don't have. Everything a privilege, nothing n entitlement.

ay no heed. I'm full of crap. You lot are worse for reading and heeding

Monday, 29 February 2016

We are at a posh hotel for a spa weekend, the Hells Bells is getting a facial, I'm for massage.

We went down to the relaxation area to wait. It's a busy spot. Everyone else is potless in white hotel dressing gowns and white hotel slippers. I'm unshaven and wearing a golf shirt, jeans and runners. The treatment ladies silently appeared one y one. You would suddenly look up and there one was.

Emma, she whispered.

Off Emma went.

Another one magically appeared.

Sarah, she whispered.

Off Sarah went.

Hells Bells was whispered.

Off Hells Bells went, silently, smoothly.

Then I heard a thud of a footstep.

And another one.

And another.

The lemon infused water quivered.

The steps got closer.

They got louder.

A huge arm appeared.

A huge shock of bleach blond hair appeared.

The rest of it appeared.

My name was called.

It was roared from the door, in a big deep voice.

There was no tiptoeing or whispering here. I looked around me.

I was hoping someone else would jump up.

No one volunteered.

That's me says me.

For a massage loike she says.

She didn't say massage with the French inflection, she said massage like a mayo man would say message.

That's me says me.
She looked me up and down.
She nodded approvingly.
She put her hands together and cracked her knuckles.
C'mon ahead she thundered.
I followed meekly.

She wasn't from Mayo. She was a Rossie, from Roscommon. She told me as
played this little piggy with my toes. She told me not to bother with any of the
shite in the shop loike, it's much chayper on cue vee see. She split up with her
partner and loike she's happy but loike sometimes it's hard. She said loike a lot.
She worked my hamstrings and then told me to roll over on my back. She held up
the towel covering me as I turned to stop it catching. She held it up quite high. She
held it up very high. She held it right out of the way. I'm glad I kept my cacks on.
She seemed disappointed.

Next time Im getting a massage Im going to ask for a Rossie massage. It really was
that good.

Wednesday, 16 March 2016
I like quirky.
I like oddball.
I like different.
I like people that sing 'we built the pyramids' when watching Big Bang.
I like the magic road in Cooley.
I like the pyramid in Garvagh.
I like the jumping church in Killdemock.
I like the magic river in Fore.
I like that there is a place called Fore.
I like the tragic tale of Fr Pat Noise.
I like the Echo gate in Meath.
I like the wonderful barn in Kildare.
I like the unfinished musical bridge in Mayo.
I like the Connemara giant, carved for no apparent reason.
I like the ghost face in Ballycastle.
I like the shoe tree in Islandmagee, sadly no more.
I like the wizards grave in Cushendun. Or maybe it's Cushendall.
They are just quirky.
I like quirky.
Sameness is boring.
Conformity is boring.
Don't be boring.
Hope you all have a quirky day.

riday, 25 March 2016

started the effin motorbike last night for the first time since December. I charged
p the battery and let her rip in the garage. It was a bit smoky but in my defence i
idn't expect it to start. It doesn't usually start. As soon as it started I opened the
oor to let the smoke out. It was lovely. It was like an old friend coming home
fter a long time away. I was happy.

knew that the Hells Bells wouldn't be just as happy as me.
he Hells Bells doesn't love the wee bike like only a biker can.
walked in and sat down beside her.
he sniffed.
he sniffed gain.
smell smoke she says.
smiled like an eejit.
he thought about it.
t's that effin bike she says.
You started it she says.
n the bloody garage she says.
With the bloody door closed she says.
he house will stink she says.
just smiled like an eejit. I find smiling like an eejit gets me out of many tricky
ituations.
he went into the kitchen.
The smell was worse out there.
he uttered a profanity.
was shocked.
A profanity that even if I could spell it I couldn't write in this.
he opened the door to the back hall towards the garage.
he took the name of our Lord God in vain.
just smiled like an eejit.

Monday, 11 April 2016

had to take wee daughter to school this morning. I used to drive her every day but
she now drives herself. She couldn't drive herself today so I did. Ive missed these
mornings.

I turned the radio on.
I started to sing along.
She told me to stop singing.
I tapped along with the music instead.
She gave me a look.

I stopped tapping.
I lifted my hand to blow my nose.
She grunted at me.
I turned it into a nose scratch instead.
She gave another grunt.
I turned it into a hair fix type movement starting at my nose.
She gave up.
I got chirpy seeing all the school commuters I haven't seen in a while.
I waved at a few.
It suddenly got frosty in the car.
I beeped at the friend that's a boy.
I beeped at the friend that's a bus driver.
I got told off. Though shalt not beep.
I got emotional seeing the teachers' cars that I haven't seen in months.
I got told to wise up.
I dropped her off in the teachers' car park.
I got told off.
I waved and smiled at the friend that's a boy on the way out. She wasn't there to tell me off. I didn't beep in case she heard me. Thou shalt not beep.
I've missed those morning aggravating my wee girl. Today was brilliant. I hope she wants a lift tomorrow. :-)

Wednesday, 13 April 2016
There is a problem.
I'm attempting Cycle against Suicide cycle around Ireland.
Its two weeks on the bike starting 24th April.
The problem was pointed out by Pops with some delight.
24th April 2016 is also census day.
It happens every 5 years.
Every person in Ireland is recorded and logged and analysed on census day.
I will be staying overnight in Virginia, County Cavan.
For those who don't know Cavan lads have a reputation for being a bit tight.
They say Lough Neagh was formed when a Cavan man dropped a penny in a puddle and went looking for it.
For the next 5 years, the Government will hold my census records as a Cavan man and a Virgin.

Sunday, 17 April 2016
I was away yesterday cycling. I dressed in cycling gear and left home early. I stopped in Applegreen on the M1 outside Belfast for breakfast. I was standing at the till getting served. At the other till was a huge muscular man with a sloping forehead and a regularly broken misshapen nose. His wee sheepish wife stood

ehind him. He had to pay by card, and he was brought over to my till. He bumped is way in, without as much as a pardon me or a scuzemee (Nordie for Excuse me). his irritated me. His wife apologised for him. This irritated me more. He gave her dirty look. This further irritated me.

ou know the way sometimes it only takes 5 seconds to realise that he is a big upid cunning insecure bully, and she is constantly being put down in small ways ver and over and over for years and years and years? I knew this immediately.

went over to the counter to put milk in the tea. He was already there. He slopped ie milk in, spilling some on the floor. He spilt sugar all over the counter. He umped the sugar wrappers on the floor beside the bin. Her face didn't change.

Ie turned to me.
ioing riding he says?
ye says me.
Ve were riding yesterday he says.
Vere you says me?
ye we were riding all night he says with a guffaw.
Ier face didn't change.
Do you know the way you automatically think at times like this to say nothing and walk away?
didn't think.
Your missus doesn't look happy says me.
You mustn't be very good at it says me.
Ier face may have changed.
Or I may have imagined it.
His face certainly changed.
drew myself to my full height, and casually but quickly left in my cycling long John's with the big padded arse, with my head up high, and my dignity intact.

Sunday, 24 April 2016

Cycle Against Suicide day 1 takes us from Phoenix park Dublin to Virginia with a lunch stop in Navan. We heard from a single mum with 4 kids and a full-time job that has run a marathon then a triathlon then an iron-man then a double iron-man while battling cancer and having massive tumours removed. She is now training to do 1100kms in 74 hours on the bike. Respect.

I've been told that I'm not perfect, I never was and I never will be. Accept it. Neither are you. Accept it.

I've been told that I have made balls ups, and I will make them in future. Live with it. So will you. Live with that too.

I've been told that peoples opinion of me just isn't valid, neither is mine of them. So, get on with it.

I met a mummy whose young daughter Jen has just been readmitted to hospital suffering from depression. She just can't shake it. And her and her mate still came on the cycle for the morning. That's how much #CASuicide800 means to them. Oh and #CASuicide800 is apparently trending. I haven't a clue what that means but apparently it's quite cool. Trend away please.

Oh, and Navan Mazda which had the best EVER radio advert in the Zoom Zoom Mazda era is now a Kia and Mercedes dealer. That a shame.

Oh, and people from Virginia are called Virginians, not Virgins. So, on the census I'm a Virginian. Quite impressed with that.

Cavan to Monaghan tomorrow. #itsoknottobeok.

Monday, 25 April 2016.

Its day two of Cycle Against Suicide, Virginia to Monaghan via Cavan town. We were in Virginia college this morning, a school assembly with 700 kids and their teachers. The kids all washed and scrubbed and hair done like it's first day back after the holidays. Everything spick and span for the visitors off the television. They were sitting on the floor neatly in rows, sorted by class. The wee ones to the front, older ones to the back, short ones nearest the centre aisle, planned to perfection. The troublemakers kept in an isolation area to the back right. They were beside the fire exit for a quick evacuation and surrounded by some of the more militant teachers. The teachers were armed with chalk board dusters for throwing and metre rulers for poking.

We just know that mammies have threatened the wooden spoon to the kids and ordered them to behave and not be showing the Virginians up in front of the posh people from the big smoke. We know that the teachers have warned them to behave because we are going to Monaghan next, and they wouldn't want the cyclists to think to Cavan ones are culchies. There they sat, like a scene of perfection from OCD weekly.

Then the force of nature that is Jim Breen came in. And in 10 seconds they were screaming and shouting and letting it all out with Will-I-am and Britney Britney while bouncing round the hall. And the teachers glowering at him so he got them up to dance too. The headmaster glowered at the teachers so even he got dragged in. We cyclists were standing at the back enjoying the show, so he got us up to dance too. Pandemonium. In a Virginia school hall. In County Cavan. At 10am. Monday morning.

Then there was a chat, a few speeches, some by the kids, for the kids and the adults. I'm not going to relate what was said. If you want to know get on your bike and join in. Today I saw 699 kids spontaneously, out of the blue, unprompted give a standing ovation to a one of their own suffering from demons.

he kids did you proud Virginia mammies and teachers. This posh person from the
ig smoke is very impressed.

uesday, 26 April 2016
s day 3 of Cycle Against Suicide, and its Monaghan to Portadown for lunch to
ookstown.
was chatting to a fellow cyclist.
Ve went through the formalities.
Vhere are you from?
4ow many days are you doing?
Vhy are you doing it she says?
)on't know says me.
)on't know she says?
)on't know says me.
´ou must know she says.
have an idea says me.
have 10 ideas says me.
3ut I don't have a main reason says me.
Vhat's number 1 idea she says?
)on't know says me.
)on't know she says?
)on't know says me.
)o you always avoid answering questions she says?
)on't know says me.
)on't start that again she says.
3tart what says me?
)on't know says she.
We laughed.

3o why are you doing it says me?
3he didn't pause.
3he didn't think about it.
3he just replied.

For all those who suffer alone.

Wednesday, 27 April 2016
We were travelling down the road, towards a wee primary school on the left. There
were lots of kids out at the wall. They came out to wave and cheer us past. I saw
the Tarmac on the hard shoulder the whole way to the wall. My immediate thought
was high five.
I roared it. HIGH FIVE.

I swerved left.
They all perked up.
They all leaned out.
They all reached out.
Then I thought what if I crash?
What if I hit the wall?
What if one of them has heavy hands?
There could be carnage.
I careered down along the wall one handed high fiving as many as I could.
I was very proud of my efforts.

At the end was a wee teacher in her 40s, hairstyle from the 60s and Deirdre Barlow glasses from the 80s. You know the type. Every school has one. She wasn't smiling. She didn't seem amused. She was giving me the look. But I was doing 15mph and I was feeling brave.
I gave her the nod.
At the very last second she gave me a wee shy shrug of resignation and she raised her hand.
She raised it out far enough to make me reach for a high 5 but not far enough to be brazen about it.
We high fived.
Down went her hand before any students could see it.

I value people like that. Maybe they don't quite fit in. Maybe they don't want to. Maybe clothes or hairstyle or behaviour not quite up to date or trendy or sophisticated. But I find those are the exact people you want on your side when times get tough.

Tuesday, 26 April 2016
So anyway, I have a bit of whimsy for you at last. We were in Portadown. We were about to leave. We were getting the pep talk and the safety talk from the Marshall. The Marshalls are brilliant by the way. I have never been yelled at by nicer people.

The Marshall told us that the route was flat, but there was a very strong headwind, all the way to Coalisland. It is open country with no shelter. He advised us to tuck in behind someone big and let them break the wind. He advised us to keep close, right on their back wheel, tucked right in under their arse. It would make it a lot easier.

I looked around for someone big to target. I looked at the group ahead. I looked at the group behind. I wondered why everyone was looking at me and giving me the thumbs up and smiling.

have never felt as loved as I was at that moment.

Wednesday, 27 April 2016

Day 4 of Cycle against suicide today, Cookstown to Omagh to Stranolar.

I promised to post an update every night, so I will keep that promise. Even though today was shite.

I started brilliantly in Cookstown in the school hall. There was a gang of big Tyrone teenage lads that just know everything there is to know about everything, watching a gang of auld lads in cycling short and orange tops dancing and jumping about and telling them they are wrong. Then Jim Breen starts talking. They listen with bemused curiosity. Shortly into it there is the moment when the mood changes. It sweeps across the kids. Curiosity becomes intensity. They sit up, they stop fidgeting, they edge forward, they start considering and they start getting the message.

We left, and what a fantastic exit from the schools in Cookstown. We were heading for Carrickmore when the sleet hit us, and rain, and wind. Then it turned white. I took a dizzy spell, had a fall, and ended up on the sweeper bus, then in the ambulance then back on the bus. I have a chest infection, not bad but no cycling for a few days.

The bus is crap. You get straight on, and straight down the back to get the anger out. Feckin doctor. Feckin weather. Feckin Carrickmore. Feckin potholes. You get it out of your system. You feel sorry for yourself. You get emotional. You get maudlin. You are feeling rough. You are feeling rotten. You are feeling like a failure. Then you wise up. You realise it isn't about the half day that you haven't done, it's actually about the three and a half days you have done. You move up to the middle and join in the craic. You realise that there is nothing to be ashamed of. Someone else gets on. They are feeling crap. You give them a round of applause. They go down the back. You know how they are feeling. You chat to your neighbour. You realise the bus isn't that bad.

I'm gutted. I'm totally and utterly peeved and pished and fecked off and miffed and disappointed. However its ok not to be ok.

Thursday, 28 April 2016

I've had an epiphany.
I've had a vision.

I've had a sudden moment of great revelation and realisation, clarity of thought and imagination. The world has become clearer, brighter, bluer, oranger.

I fell yesterday at a lovely wee woman's house outside Carrickmore. I sat on her spotless step. Gleaming it was from years of scrubbing.
Do ya wanna drink a wat'r shun she says?
That's the way they say water up round there. They rush it. Wat'r.
No thanks says me.
Or a cup a tae she says?
My ears perked up. My interest was piqued at the tae. I reckon her tae would be great. But I didn't have time. The ambulance was coming. I declined.

Anyway, the epiphany. It's not far away from me. It's just down the road. I can finish that day anytime. In June. Or July. I can walk up her spotless step and knock on her door and say I'm here for me tae. She did offer. And then cycle to Omagh, then to Stranolar. And then I can do the Donegal day. I can take over the whole of the town. I can high 5 all the pedestrians on the way in. I can say thanks to all the Police and Guards. I can shout SLOWING and HOLE LEFT even though I'm on my own, in my Orange CAS jacket, that I'm very proud of.

Onwards and upwards lads, I'm going to do the 14 days, I'm just not going to do them in a row. Cancel the holidays Hells Bells, you are driving the support bus! This is going to be a busy summer!!! #CASuicide800.

Saturday, 30 April 2016
The will be the last day of Cycle Against Suicide for me for a bit.

While I feel like I have the miles in the legs and the hills have been manageable, the weather at 1 degree for cycling has beaten me. I picked up a nasty throat infection on Tuesday, I got a ride in an ambulance Wednesday, and I headed home Wednesday night. I saw my own doctor Thursday morning. He called me back Thursday afternoon. He then sent me to A&E in Antrim. They wanted to admit me, but had no beds. I told them I was going home, I was off work, and I was going to put my feet up and rest. They insisted on complete rest. The ordered me to stay out of the cold. The advised me to wrap up warm. The insisted on no strenuous activity. And under those conditions they discharged me. As long as I promised not to cycle. Si I promised and went home.

Next morning, Friday, I re-joined the cycle with the wee daughter in Bundoran. It was a beautiful day with beautiful scenery. Bundoran to Manorhamilton with views of Benbulben and the Glencar waterfall. It was amazing to have Emma beside me, until she took off and left me and my infection riddled wheezing. And we are going to do this afternoon Saturday from Boyle to Carrick on Shannon. And en sadly I'm calling it a day. I'm going to belatedly take the doctor's advice. It's nly fair. I did promise.

was once asked whether I did do something good today. I'm going to be able to nswer yes. Every day this week, except Thursday. Thursday I looked a lovely wee octor called Kevin in A&E Antrim in the eye and promised him faithfully that I as going home to rest. I assured him that I wasn't re-joining the cycle. I lied. I nink he knew I was lying. I think he understood.

afe travelling lads. #itsoknottobeok. Hopefully see you in Waterford. Failing that Vexford. But definitely Arklow for the last day to Dublin. Even if I'm completely anjaxed I'm going to Arklow. Just don't tell wee Kevin in A&E.

aturday, 7 May 2016

o anyway, I'm back on the Cycle against suicide. Don't tell Nathan, the aramedic. He won't be happy. I got ill last week. I tested Nathan's patience by ticking around and cycling when I really wasn't fit. He got quite irate but nankfully and to his credit stopped short of chucking me off. This time I have aken precautions. I have got some orange hair colouring so he won't recognise me.

ast Wednesday I ended up on the bus in the afternoon. Not by choice. I viewed it s wasted time. I was disappointed. Upset. Frustrated. Grumpy. Gutted.
onight, in the pub a lady came up to me.
Hiya she says.
Do you remember me she says?
spoke to you on the bus she says.
ast Wednesday she says.
Omagh to Ballybofey she says.
enjoyed our chat she says.
t meant a lot to me she says.
t made a difference she says.

t made a difference to me too.
'm chuffed that I was there.
I'm chuffed that she chatted to me.
So maybe it wasn't wasted time. Maybe I shouldn't have been so grumpy and miffed. Next time I will try harder not to let little thinks like a spin on a sweeper ous get to me.

Arklow to Dublin tomorrow for the big finish. Stay safe.

#CASuicide800. #itsoknottobeok.

Monday, 9 May 2016

I'm driving down the M2 in Belfast.
I'm missing the Cycle Against Suicide.
I'm missing the orange.
I'm missing the high fives.
I'm missing the beeping and cheering and waving and yee hawing.
I'm missing the quiet moments when people tell you their story.
I'm missing the photos.
I'm missing the schools.
I'm missing the downhills.
I'm missing the HOLE LEFT!!

I reached the end of the Motorway.
I put down my window.
I put my arm straight out and up.
And I roared SLOWING at the top of my considerable voice.

And I smiled to myself. Take care lads.

Thursday, 12 May 2016

I went into the Mace for a bowl of stew. The stew is 2 quid. I got 2 bottles of coke zero. The Coke Zero was £1.39 each. I went to the till to pay. There is a big lad serving, he isn't quite right, he is slightly awkward and a wee touch slow. You know the type.

He rang the bits through. £4.78.
You know he says we have Coke Zero cans on special.
6 cans for 2 pound he says.
That's..... that's.... he started to do the sums.....in his head but out loud.... 6 cans at 330 ml each.... 3 cans is one litre... 6 cans is two litres..... that's 2 litres for 2 pound he proclaimed.
And you are getting 2 bottles he says.
At 500 ml each he says.
That's only 1 litre he says.
For £2.78 he says.
You would be better with the cans he advised with delight.
Grand says me.
I will take the cans so says me.
I got the cans. He rang them through.
£6.78 he said proudly.
Oh, take the bottles off says me.
I don't need them now says me.

...e was aghast. He had big sad eyes.
...ve already rung them through he says.
...h OK then says me smiling in apology.
...m not allowed to do cancellations he says.
...ure, I will take them says me.
...will have to get the boss he says.
...on't worry its grand says me.
...ure, you can drink them anyway he says.
You're right says me,
...will take them says me.
...will drink them anyway says me.
...is face lit up. He was happy again.
...6.78 he said proudly.
...an I have a bag says me.
...or my 3 litres of Coke zero says me.
...have to charge he says.
6.83 he says.
...o I paid him £7.
...tick the rest in the jar says me.
And off I went.

...like shops like that. I like businesses that give people a chance. I like businesses
...hat take a wee risk on people. People that otherwise might struggle to hold down a
...ob. Here's the barmy bit. I reckon I've just been steered and scammed by a big lad
...vith learning difficulties. But I loved it. I'm going back tomorrow. I hope the
...andit is working. I hope he fleeces me again.

Anyone want a drink? I've got Coke Zero??

Thursday, 19 May 2016
I'm at my mammy's house.
You know you are in your mammy's house when the dishwasher has 16 cups from
all the tea.
And 2 plates from last night's dinner.

Friday, 20 May 2016
I was driving down the road past me old primary school. I saw me mammy out
walking. She was chatting to a man. I stopped to say hello.
Hi mammy says me.
Well son she says, do you remember this man?
I did. It was my old headmaster. I couldn't remember his name. I remember his
nickname, Kelloggs. I couldn't call him that. I remember his first name too, Jim.
But I couldn't call him that either.

Hello sir says me.
Young man he says.
You've put on a bit of weight he says.
I put my head down.
Yes sir mutters me.
Speak up he says.
Don't mutter he says.
Sorry sir mutters me.
Sort that out he says.
Yes sir says me.
Bye sir says me.
Bye mammy says me.

Off I went to Belfast. I was glad to get out of there.

I was at half way home when i remembered he was Mr Kelleher and he was my primary school headmaster. I last saw him when I was 12.

A bit of weight. Once a headmaster, always a headmaster.

Sunday, 29 May 2016
I was pouring wine for the Hells Bells.
Say when says me.
I poured.
And poured.
And poured.
And eventually stopped after about a gallon.
I didn't say when she says.

You want some Twirl Bites says me.
Aye she says.
Say when says me.
I poured some into her bowl.
And poured.
And poured.
Bollox. She got me again.

Tuesday, 14 June 2016
I'm sitting in a wee cafe in Bridge Street Belfast having a cuppa. I am being served by a wee tubby blond waitress. She could be aged anywhere from early 40s to late 50s. Knowing Me Knowing You by ABBA is on the radio. She was singing along. The chef in the kitchen is singing along too. He has a very fine voice, he has a church voice. Its loud and strong and proud and unashamed. I'm the only customer.

ne was clearing the table opposite. She lifted the two plates, two cups, a teapot
nd milk, and did a perfect 360 spin followed by a left leg drag. And then gave me
ne dirtiest most suggestive wink I've ever received. It's a little piece of pure joyful
nagic on a wet Tuesday morning in Belfast while the people in the bus queue to
Monkstown outside stand facing away and completely oblivious.

love people like that. I love characters. Good morning Belfast. You're in good
orm today......

Monday, 20 June 2016

was Father's Day yesterday. I had a great day, thanks.

left wee daughter into work and really enjoyed spending that 20 minutes with her.
hose times have become scare where she started driving. It was lovely.

big son came home from Newcastle and we all just hung out and chatted in the
fternoon. Those times have become scarce too. It was lovely.

Ve went to see Pops for Father's Day, and catch up with the Aussies and the big
ro and the wee bro and the various boys and girls and men and ladies. It doesn't
appen often enough. It was lovely.

hen we came home. All went to bed. I sat up. I watched the golf. With a glass of
vine. And a snack. The house settled down for the night. I had the lights off. And
ne volume low. And I thought about how lucky I am. It was lovely.

And then I thought of those friends and family who no longer have their father on
Father's Day.

Friday, 24 June 2016
The Hells bells went to Majorca last Tuesday.
The UK voted to leave Europe yesterday.
How will she get home?
Will she get back in?
Am I now effectively single?
Should I change my Facebook status?

Tuesday, 28 June 2016
My wee motorbike is very sick.
It doesn't look good.
It may be terminal.

The motorbike doctor can't fix it.
It's waiting for an appointment with the big doctor.
If he can't fix it that's it.
We are out of options.
Home for some family time before the trip to the big scrapyard up high.
I'm upset.
I'm gutted.
We've had some good times, the wee motorbike and me.
But there is still hope.
It's a fighter.
I'm keeping my fingers crossed.
I'm lighting candles.

The Hells Bells?
She's keeping her fingers crossed too.
She's desperately hoping that the effin bike will never recover.
She is over the moon.
She can't stop smiling.
She's finding it hard to sit still.
Every day she asks for news.
With a nervous worried face.
And every day I tell her it's not good.
And her face eases and a grin appears.........

Sunday 3 July 2016.
I did the 180km Ring of Kerry charity cycle yesterday. I was cycling up
Coomakista. Coomakista is not an especially high hill, it's not an especially steep
hill, but it's just a long drawn out drag of a pull with no respite for 8k after
Waterville. A skinny lad wearing colour matched bike and shoes and clothes and
gloves went past me. I was panting and wheezing and sweating and huffing and
puffing in my golf t-shirt and office socks.

Have you ever instantly disliked someone? Have you ever felt instant pure and
deep irrational hatred? That's what I felt. If I could have caught him I could have
killed him right then. But while we were going uphill he was perfectly safe.

We eventually got to the top where all the gang high fived each other and took the
annual selfie on the top of Coomakista. That is the half way point of the cycle. I
forgot all about him. We looked at the view, we marvelled on how far we had
come, we celebrated how a load of lads from a small parish on the North-East
coast could gather together on the of a hill on the South-West coast. All was good
again.

'e took off down the other side. Suddenly in front of me I saw what looked like
e back end of an Iceland frozen chicken in colour matching clothes and bike and
noes. It was the skinny lad that passed me on the way up. He had the head down
nd the arse up and pedalling like a demon. Now I have a bit more ballast than
im. And on the uphill I really suffer because of it. It all has to be brought from the
ottom to the top, and all in one trip. But on the downhill gravity help the ballast
nd there is no hope of slowing me.

free wheeled past him while he was in the crouch and pedalling like a demon
had one hand on the handlebars. I was sitting fully upright. I was facing left
owards him.
ood man says me.
eep her lit says me.
Vords to that effect.
latitudes to him.
atronising to him.
m not proud of myself.
ut it felt really really good.

freewheeled for miles and miles towards Sneem. As soon as I hit an uphill I
ulled in to change my coat. I hid behind a hedge. There was no way was i letting
nat skinny lad in the colour matched equipment know he had passed me again.

Ring of Kerry? It was gas craic altogether. See you next year.

Tuesday, 5 July 2016.
'm outlet shopping in the Kildare outlet shopping.
t's where gobshites go to shop.
The lady in front of me has just proclaimed that her bra is her best friend. Its
hopping for that sort of gobshite.
went up to a security guard. Standing to attention.
He didn't look at me.
He looked like a big thick Dub.
n that big thick way that only big thick Dubs can pull off.
His expression never changed.
Any bookshops here says me?
No, he says.
DIY shops says me?
No, he says.
Golf shops says me?
No, he says.
Anything of any interest or any use to me in here whatsoever says me?
Yeah, he says.
What says me?

Starbucks, he replied

He grinned. I grinned too.
Good man says me.
You fancy a coffee says me?
Thanks, he says.
But I'm not allowed he says.

I brought him one anyway. He is the only sensible lad in the place.

Wednesday, 13 July 2016
The Hells Bells is having cheese. Wensleydale with cranberry and smoked
Applewood. She is having it with nice multi flavour crackers and a glass of chilled
prosecco.

I too am having cheese. Wensleydale with cranberry and smoked Applewood also.
I however am having it with thickly buttered digestives, a bag of Tayto cheese and
onion (southern Tayto of course) and a pint of chilled Miwadi orange.

Women. Strange creatures. Odd as bejaysus.

Wednesday, 13 July 2016
I get asked regularly why Cycle Against Suicide means so much to me. There are
several reasons. Some of the reasons are not my place to share. So, I deflect the
question. A big part of it however is the people you meet. I'm going to give you an
example.

I was sitting on a outside at lunchtime. I was having a bit of down time. I was in a
beautiful place looking over water at a hill opposite. An older quiet man came and
sat beside me. The type of man that observes and enjoys but doesn't really
participate. Bit distant. Bit reserved. We munched and sat.

It's great to be alive he said.
This was out of the blue, no prompting from me.
Aye says me.
In total and utter agreement.
We munched away.
A minute or two went by.
I couldn't have said that two years ago he said.
Aye? says me leaving the door open for more.
Aye he says.
We munched on.

Another minute or two went by.
Couldn't have said it last year he said.
Aye? says me again leaving the door slightly ajar.
He munched on.
Can say it now he says.
Aye says me approvingly.
He finished the grub.
He stretched out and leaned back.
He watched the world go by.
Then he balled up his rubbish.
He got up.
Thanks for the chat he says.
You're a great man for the chat.
And away he went.
Another minute or two went by.
Aye says me in total and utter agreement.
itsoknottobeok. #CASuicide800.
He was right. It is indeed great to be alive.

Wednesday, 20 July 2016

Anyway 16 years ago today I was at a wedding in the Carrickdale Hotel. The reception was on the big room on the right if you are travelling south. My wee sister was getting married.

When the bride and indeed the groom left without saying goodnight to me I got a bit emotional. I have a habit of doing that at times. I went outside to get some air. I wandered down a corridor and out the fire escape. I ended up in the garden, all alone except for my pint. I had a bit of down time. I had a bit of quiet time.

I went to get back in after a few minutes. The fire escape had closed behind me. I could see the party going on strong 40 feet away through another glass door. No matter how hard i knocked and kicked and banged the door no one looked my way. I went around towards the main door on the Northern side of the building. There was a big wrought iron fence closing off the garden, and the gate was locked.

I went back the way I came. I knocked on the fire escape door again on the way past. No one missed me. I went around the south side. There was another wrought iron fence with another locked gate. But this side had a wee wall below it to enable me to get a leg up. I put my pint on the wall and climbed up and over the gate. I then reached through for my pint. The pint wouldn't fit through the gap in the fence. The bars were too close together. I had to pass the pint from hand to hand along the wrought iron fence until I reached a fancy part with twirls which was

slightly wider and there I could pass the pint through. The fence is still there today
I smile every time I pass it.

I walked back into the reception, only to meet the bride and groom who hadn't
actually left. The groom looked at me coming back in covered in rust stains and
paint flakes.
How did you get out past us he says?
I dodged the question.
I just walked out there now says me.
You were talking says me.
You didn't see me says me.
He was suspicious. He did that sideways nod narrow eyes thing. But he let it go.
As did I.

We were all sitting together at breakfast the next morning. The maître d came over
I had never met him before.
He was a swarthy lad with deep meaningful eyes.
Morning Sir he says to me, in front of everyone.
Morning says me puzzled.
The bride looked at me curiously.
Did you get in all right last night he says?
I did says me more puzzled.
The bride listened intently.
Good man he says.
We were worried about you climbing the fence there he says.
The brides mouth gaped.
But then we saw the state of you and figured you had to be one of the family so we
just let you be he says.
I had to own up.
Thanks, Maître d, which I believe is French for Tout.

Anyway happy 16th anniversary Aine and Paul.
The wedding was gas.
I really enjoyed it.

PS The fence is only 5 feet high. I could have lifted the pint over it, instead of
passing it along hand to hand. I didn't realise at the time. Go check if you don't
believe me. Carrickdale Hotel. On the right.

Friday, 22 July 2016
Do you want a wee feel good story? On a wet Friday morning in Belfast? To cheer
you up? You do? OK then.

Carrickfergus Senior Gateway is a social and educational club for people with learning difficulties. The members are among the most deprived, most discriminated against, the most in need in our society. They struggle with almost every aspect of life. This wee club staffed by volunteers provides a very valuable outlet for them and their carers. Sadly, like every other charitable organisation, they are in need of funds, of volunteers and of carers. The always are. They probably always will be.

They came into a few pounds recently. Not a huge amount. A nice amount. And they decided to put it towards a defibrillator, and site it outside. They used the money for the whole of the town.

So basically, the most desperate, most needy, most deprived people in our society get a wee windfall. And they immediately give it away. To help others. How bloody fantastic is that?

Friday, 29 July 2016
I'm out of the proper Tayto.
It's a disaster.
I can go and get some of the Nordie stuff but it's just not the same.
I need the good stuff.
The uncut stuff.
I need to go on a Tayto run.
I need to cross the border.
I need to take an unapproved road.
I need to follow the fuel tankers.
I need to fill the boot with proper Tayto.
I need to avoid the customs on the way back.
I need to fill the spare wheel well.
I need to stuff some under the seats.
Hide a bag or two in the glovebox.
Sprinkle pepper to foil the sniffer dogs.
Those custom feckers always claim they are dipping for red diesel or looking for cigarettes, but I know they are actually looking for the Tayto.
If they catch me I will be in the Sunday World like Michaela.
They claim she was carrying drugs to Peru.
I reckon she was carrying the Tayto.
Flash the lights if the customs are dipping.
I will pull in and swallow the evidence.
I believe they call it ingesting.
I better get some diet coke to wash it all down.
If the customs annoy me I will just ingest them too.

Saturday, 30 July 2016

Myself and the Hells Bells were having a chat.

What do you want to do today she says?

I had a moment of worry.

I don't like it when she asks my opinion.

I'm not used to it.

She normally just tells me my opinion and I go with the flow, or ignore it and do what I want, so asking me is kind of irrelevant.

What do you want to do says me?

I need to go to Asda she says.

OK says me, I will go golfing for a few hours and then we will put the boat in this afternoon and then meet up with the lads at some point later says me.

OK she says.

Do you want to let the lads know the plans says me?

I already did she says.

Half an hour ago she says.

So it didn't matter what I said, the plans were made anyway says me?

No, she says, but it's nice that you agree.

I'm tempted to change the plans to show my contempt at the disrespect, but I really want to go golfing.

Tuesday, 2 August 2016

Do you want to hear about three people that impressed me? A young couple and their wee daughter?

Last weekend we were sitting in Francos, our favourite restaurant in Enniskillen. We had been out on the water all day, so as usual we were wind burned and scruffy. That doesn't seem to matter in Francos.

A young couple came in beside us. They had a wee girl in a large buggy. We shifted seats to give them a bit more room.

No need they says.

It's grand sure we are moved now says me.

That's lovely thanks they says.

Here take the chair away and get the buggy tucked in says me.

No need they says.

Sure take this chair away too says me.

And we got the buggy in nice and tight.

We got chatting.

In the buggy was Charlie.

Charlie is not her real name, but it should have been.

She looked like a Charlie.

Charlie was 7.

Charlie had muscular dystrophy.

Charlie couldn't walk or talk but she loved movement and colours.

Charlie wasn't expected to live past 5, but here was Charlie was out and about and living it large in Fermanagh.

Charlie was wearing a lovely blue top and white leggings.

Charlie had beautiful shiny shoes and a lovely bracelet.

She had her nails painted and her hair shining and set lovely.

Mummy and Daddy were dressed to impress too.

That wee family were having a wee night out, and they were going to enjoy it.

It was Charlie's painted nails that impressed me most in a strange way. The effort that had been made to show off this young lady on a night out impressed me, to dress to impress and do hair and makeup and nails. We personally know how difficult it can be, and how much easier it is to grab a takeaway and sit in. But this wee family were out and about.

They brought their own food for Charlie.

It had no lumps, because Charlie had trouble swallowing.

They asked apologetically if chef wouldn't mind heating it up.

Chef was very glad to oblige.

Mummy fed Charlie.

She turned Charlie so that Charlie could see all the comings and goings in a busy restaurant.

I played peek a boo with the wine bottle until mummy gave me that sigh that says enough now.

The sigh that says this child needs to eat.

I know that sigh well.

I get that sigh from lots of mummy's.

The waitresses and grinned and waved as they went past.

They made sure to go past again.

And again.

Pizza Chef leaned out of the pizza kitchen and waved the big spatula thing for moving pizzas and almost clunked a waitress.

Charlie smiled. I laughed. Mummy sighed again.

I wanted to tell mummy not to sigh at me, that it was all chefs fault, but it wasn't an aggressive sigh. It was a sigh of resignation. It was a sigh of OK you win.

Mummy and Daddy ordered their meal. One starter between them. A main course each.

Their starter arrived.

Mummy put Charlie in her buggy.

I was sorry to see her go.

So were the waitresses.

The atmosphere dropped.

It clouded over.

Daddy immediately lifted Charlie back out.
Mummy sighed. That resignation sigh again. That sure what are you going to do sigh.
I was happy.
So were the waitresses.
So was the chef.
The buzz lifted again.
Dad also turned her so she could see the busy room.
Mummy ate the starter.
Daddy nibbled.
Charlie smiled.
I smiled.
The Hells Bells smiled.
The waitresses smiled.

The main courses arrived.
Mummy tucked in.
Daddy nibbled.
Then mummy took Charlie and nibbled and again let her face the room, while daddy ate the rest of his meal.
Meanwhile every waitress grinned and waved.
Charlie smiled.
The barman pretended to trip while carrying a tray.
Charlie smiled.
I pretended to be a fish swimming through the condiments and the prosecco bottle I did the bubble noises. I don't know why. It seemed the right thing to do.
Charlie smiled. And smiled. And smiled.

Don't give me this crap about young ones today being soft and lazy, because they are not. I have proof.
Don't give me this shite about some people not making a contribution to society because everybody makes a contribution. Loving, lovable, loved. I have proof.
Don't give me this shite about a lack of community spirit in modern times, because it's there if you look for it. I found it.

Anyway, well done to Francos and staff for giving us all great meal and a better attitude, as always. And thanks to Mummy and Daddy for painting Charlie's nails and making her pretty and for sitting her on your knee so she could see the room and we could see her. And thanks to Charlie. For smiling. And turning a quiet quick pizza into a meal i will smile about for a long time.

Good morning Fermanagh. It's a dirty dreary wet day, but I'm feeling grand.

Tuesday, 16 August 2016

I was wandering along High street in the centre of Belfast. I don't walk fast. I don't power walk. I don't reach a gait that could be classified as urgent as a stroll. I wander. I dander. I meander.

A wee ticket seller comes up to me.

Tour bus he says?
City tour he says?
Giants Causeway he says?
Game of thrones he says?

No thanks mate says me.
I'm going to work says me.
Work shirt says me.
I'm carrying office post says me.
Brown envelopes says me.
I'm not a tourist says me.

He thought about it. He looked me up and down.
Aye but your whistling mate he says.
Workers don't whistle he says.
Tourists whistle he says.
And no offence mate he says but you look like a culchie.

He appears to be a very insightful lad. If I ever do a tour I'm going to buy a ticket from him. The bus will be full of whistling culchies. In the meantime, I'm off to get a shell suit, a Superdry t-shirt and a baseball cap. To look like a townie. Morning all.

Saturday, 20 August 2016

When we were children we used to occasionally save up our 10p pieces, get on our bikes and ride to the phone box at Thistle Cross where about 8 of us would crowd in to one phone box and phone Ardee Garda Station.
They would answer the phone 'Hello Ardee Gardai'.
We would all burst out laughing and hang up and wipe the phone box prints and ride away as fast as we could before the squad cars could get us.

Sorry Ardee Gardai.

Then one day I was listening to Cool FM in Belfast and the DJ who was from Jonesborough told almost the same story.
I'm fairly sure he wasn't in our gang. It would appear his gang were phoning Ardee Gardai too. Ardee Gardai must have had a lot of crank calls. I'm going to phone them and apologise. 04153222. I hope I don't take a fit of giggles when they answer. If I do I will hang up, wipe the phone, and run away again.

Monday, 22 August 2016

I was lying in the bed half awake.
I heard diggers out the back.
I thought that's odd on a Sunday morning.
I thought poor people living beside that on a Sunday morning.
Then the Hells Bells alarm went off.
I thought that's odd on a Sunday morning.
She hit snooze.
Then it went off again.
I thought that's odd on a Sunday morning.
She got up.
I pretended to be asleep because we have no milk.
Just as she was going out the door I said sleepily where u off to?
I have a work call she says.
I thought that's odd on a Sunday morning.
Then my alarm went off.
I thought that's odd on a Sunday morning.

That's because it's Monday. I've lost my weekend. Someone stole it.

Wednesday, 7 September 2016

I was a great child.
I only got in trouble once.
Once that I can remember.
I was selling spuds out of a small trailer at the New Inn between Dundalk and Newry.
A car stopped 50 yards away, facing north.
There was a confab in the car between man and wife.
A man got out and trotted back to me.
What spuds to you have he says.
Kerr's Pinks says me.
Balls of flour says me.
Dug up the road this morning says me.
He trotted back to the car.
There was another confab.
He trotted back to me.
Do you have any Dublin Queens he says.
No says me.
Just Kerr's Pinks says me.
All the Queens are gone two weeks ago says me.
He trotted back to the car.

There was another confab.
He trotted back to me.
There's the best place to get Dublin Queens he says.
I thought about it.
I stroked my head.
I rubbed my chin.
I will tell you the best place to get Dublin Queens says me.
You turn the car around says me.
You head in the road towards Dundalk says me.
He appeared confused.
I stopped.
Will I tell the wife says me?
Please he says.
We trotted up to the car.
I leaned in the wife's window.
Howaye missus says me.
You turn the car around says me.
They nodded eagerly.
You head in the road towards Dundalk says me.
They nodded.
You know the big bridge says me?
They nodded.
You go over that bridge says me.
You keep on that road says me.
They nodded.
Keep going 50 miles and you will reach Dublin and you can ask someone there and they will tell you says me.

The lady recognised me straightaway.
She went straight up and told me mammy.
And that was one of the few times I got in trouble.

Thursday, 8 September 2016
I got very cross a couple of weeks ago at some bullying assholes.

I was coming past the dole in Carrick, about to turn right up towards Tesco. There was a car in front of me. It was turning right too. There was a wee man on the corner waiting to cross. He was a hesitant wee man. He had a shuffling gait. He was the sort of wee man that finds everyday life a struggle.

The car in front waved him across the road.
Then the asshole let the car jump forward on the clutch to scare him.
The lads in the back found this hilarious.

The driver held up his hand by way of apology and waved the wee man across again.

He then proceeded to do the same again.

How sad can some people be, to bully a wee pensioner?

I parked and got out.

I spoke to the wee man to see if he needed a lift.

He didn't.

I tried to explain to him that the lads in front weren't trying to scare him, that they had car problems.

The car behind me also parked and came over.

The lady driving it also assured the wee man that they weren't trying to upset him

Off he went. Slowly. Nervous. Unsure. Shuffling.

Assholes. Forgive the language, but that's it already severely toned down.
Assholes.

Friday, 16 September 2016

I was bored.

I was driving to Newry along the A1.

I had just passed through the roundabout at Hillsborough.

Don't judge me too harshly.

The phone rang. I answered on handsfree.

It was an Indian lady.

Hello sir we are winging about the accident you had wecently. (Read her bit in an Indian accent pls. For effect only.)

Yes, says me.

Did you get compensation sir she says?

No says me.

I wery sorry to hear that Sir she says getting all excited.

Did you see a solicitor she says?

No says me.

Could you tell me what happened sir she says?

Why says me?

We can get you compensation sir she says.

Well says me I was standing on the footpath and my daughter in her red coupe with a yellow roof came flying down the drive and up on the footpath and hit me when I was walking and I fell and hit my head and hurt my ankle says me. (Read that bit in a culchie accent pls. For effect only)

I weally weally sorry to hear that Sir she says, but she didn't sound weally weally sorry.

I will get my supervisor sir she says, please hold.

The supervisor was on the phone quicker that I could say ok.

At this stage I was just passing Dromore.

e was an Indian gentleman.
e was even more excited than Indian lady was.
ran through the details again.
e asked my daughter's name.
told him.
hat sort of car he says?
am not sure says me, but it was a coupe, red with a yellow roof.
he accepted responsibility at the scene says me and she cried and said she was
orry says me.
nd you haven't received any compensation or seen a solicitor he asked joyfully?
o says me.
olly to hear that Sir he says again sounding anything but solly.
e took some details, address, my date of birth, accident details etc.
ould I have your daughters date of birth he says?
st January 2014 says me.
014 sir he says?
es says me.
hat would make her only 2 Sir he says puzzled?
es says me.

Oh I just remembered the name of the car says me. It was a Cosy Coupe says me.
ed says me.
ellow roof says me.
ilence.
More silence.
ou still there says me?
What about my compensation says me?
he line went dead.
didn't care.
was at Loughbrickland. Better company and craic than any radio station.

Sunday, 25 September 2016.
've just dropped my wee daughter back to university.
went in to see her room.
hoped she wouldn't get upset when I left.
didn't want tears and sobbing and a scene.
Please don't go Daddy, clinging on to my leg as I tried vainly to go down the
stairs.
Or worse the brave stoic smile with the big eyes full of tears as I left.
I resolved to drop her off and stay for 5 minutes and leave.
No fuss. No scene. Quickly and cleanly.
Which was 4 minutes more than wee daughter wanted me to stay.
This is my room she said.

And my bathroom she said.
Isn't it cute she said.
She gave me a hug.
Then she showed me out.
Bye Dad she yelled as she disappeared back down the corridor already making plans for the student union tonight.
You can let yourself out she called as the door closed in my face.

Now I'm the stoic big tear filled eyed one. Bye daughter. Proud of you. Ya wee fecker. You could have given me one tear. One measly sniffle would have made me happy. Even a rub of the nose. A sad sigh. Something. Anything......

Thursday, 29 September 2016
I was coming out of Enniskillen this morning on my way to Slieve Russell for golf I fancied a cup of tea. I stopped at the petrol station on the Sligo road just on the edge of town.
They only had Twinings tea. That's not good. I can take English tea, I'm not a bigot, despite the 700 years of occupation and all that. But Im not a fan of Twinings tea. Beggars however can't be choosers and all that
I made the tea. It was weak, and pasty, and looked sickly. I put another teabag in to try make it presentable. A wee worker came over to me.
You can't do that she snapped.
Do what says me?
You can't use two teabags she says. She was quite sharp.
Sorry says me.
She grunted at me.
Then she sighed at me.
Then I got irritated.
I took one teabag out of the water.
I lifted the wee envelope that the teabag came in.
I put the teabag back in the envelope.
I put my finger in the display box of Twinings tea bags and slid them all up an inch and pushed my teabag and envelope back in.
I did it all just to irritate her.
There ya go says me.
You can use it again says me.
Sure, it's barely damp says me.
All because she sighed at me.
She looked at me like I was stupid.
I looked back at her with big open innocent eyes and a wee happy smile on my face to confirm that yes, I actually was stupid, but that I was also quite happy in my stupidity.
She then brushed past me and took my used tea bag out and put it in the bin.

...e sighed again aggressively.

...e took a coffee sachet and opened it and put it in a cup and put the cup under the ...ee spout thing and pressed a button for hot milk.

...wasn't finished at the rather pompously called Barista Bar at this stage, I don't ...ke coffee, and I don't like sighing, grunting or aggression.

...he machine started to clank and make noise as the milk started to heat.

...he went over to the hot food counter to loudly berate the wee girl over there for ...ot filling the coffee beans.

...put a lid on my Twinings tea.

...nd because she was behind the hot food counter moaning at someone and ...ouldn't see me I put a lid on her cup that was under the spout that was just about ...o spurt a cup full of hot milk.

...he shouldn't have sighed or grunted at me.

...ff I went and paid and went to my car still smiling like I was stupid.

...he tea was actually very tasty. Sorry Twinings. I stand corrected.

...uesday, 4 October 2016

...he Hells Bells phoned me this morning at 8.11am.

...raffic is terrible she says.

...know you are heading to Belfast too she says.

...op road is heavy she says.

...went to go down Trooperslane she says.

...t was chock a block she says.

...went down Station Road in Greenisland she says.

...ig queue all the way to Whiteabbey she says.

...'m still on the M5 she says.

...was meant to start work at 8 she says.

...ou should get a motorbike says me.

...lip up the side of the traffic says me.

...e in work in plenty of time says me.

...otorbikes are great says me.

...he went all Nordie on me.

...yebutthenyouwillcrashanddieandnotbeabletolookafterthekidsyaselfishfeckerheres

...newhaaaaaseetuationjackiefullertonjimmynesbittknowwhatomeanlikesoundninety

...ightynineteyeightytheoneinthebackdidallthedamageteleteletele or words to that ...ffect.

...went back to sleep. I went onto Belfast about 10. The roads were quiet. I don't ...now what all the fuss was about. Seetuation? What seetuation?

Thursday, 6 October 2016

I'm disgusted, I'm speechless, I'm disappointed, I'm revolted, I'm upset.

I went to a garage to get breakfast. There was a wee foreign girl serving.
What can I get you she says?
Sausage beans and toast says me.
She lifted some bacon.
No bacon says me.
She lifted an egg.
No egg says me.
Sausages says me.
She lifted sausages.
Beans says me.
She lifted some beans.
Toast says me.
White or brown says she.
Oh brown please says me. She smiled approvingly.
She lifted some bread from under the counter.
Butter she says?
Yes please says me.
She buttered the bread.
Then she took the bread.
Then she put the bread in the toaster.
To toast.
With the butter already on.

Tea or coffee she says?
I was flabbergasted. I stood there with my mouth open, and a vacant expression
Tea or coffee she says?
I couldn't speak.
Tea or coffee she says a wee bit worried now.
Eh no no no thanks says me.
It's free with the breakfast she says.
No thanks says me.

I'm not going to risk tea. If that's how she makes toast, I'm not going to let her loose on a teabag.

Wednesday, 12 October 2016
I'm in the bad books so I am.
We were watching The Fall so we were.
It's about mad Nordies so it is.
I fell asleep so I did.

nd I snored so I did.
nforgiveable so it was.
 wouldn't happen with Missus Browns boys so it wouldn't.

unday, 16 October 2016
he Hells Bells and myself were sitting in alone last night.
'hat do you want to do says me?
on't know she says.
 ou want to watch a movie says me?
 ye she says.
'hat about that movie with yer man from Belfast says me.
'ho she says?
 mmy says me. Jimmy Dornan says me. From Belfast says me.
 eally? She says.
 ye says me.
 ou are going to watch that Jamie Dornan movie? she says.
 ye says me.
 reat she says. Brilliant she says. Wow she says.
he went out. She got crisps. She got prosecco. She got chocolate. For the
 omantic night in. Just the two of us and Jimmy Dornan.

 stuck on the movie. Siege of Jadotville. Grand movie. War film. With Jimmy
 ornan. As an Irish army soldier in the Congo. I enjoyed it. She seemed
 isappointed. She seemed bored. She just sat on the other chair twirling a pair
 andcuffs and playing with a whip. Can't think why.

riday, 21 October 2016
 unny story.
Wee daughter came into me this morning at 7.30.
 addy she says.
 es pet says me.
 ny chance of a lift to Mossley to get the train to Coleraine at 8.30 she says.
 es pet says me.
 o off we went at 8.10.
 dropped her off at 8.20 at Mossley train station. It's a small single track station on
 he Coleraine line.
 headed home.
My phone rang at 8.40. It was the wee daughter.
 addy she says.
Yes pet says me.
 ee the train Daddy she says.
Yes pet says me.

It didn't do to Coleraine Daddy she says.
Where did it go pet says me?
It went to Belfast Daddy she says.
Did you get the wrong train pet says me?
No Daddy she says. The wrong train got me.

Will i pick u up in Belfast in 20 mins and drive you to Coleraine pet says me?
Love you Daddy she says.
Love you too pet says me.

Friday, 28 October 2016
There is a wee lady selling the Newsletter at Applegreen on the M1 Lisburn. All
proceeds were going to the hospice. She seemed to be a lovely wee lady and it is a
great cause.
Do you want to buy a paper she says?
No says me, but I will give you the money for it.
I reached out to put a pound in her wee cup that was on top of the bench.
No stop she says.
She put her elbows out.
She had an arm full of Newsletter newspapers on one arm, and a single Newsletter
newspaper on the other arm that she was trying to give to me. This made her
efforts to stop me absurdly like she was doing the chicken dance.
I insist says me.
No stop she says still waving her elbows.
It's a great cause says me as I dropped the pound into her cup on top of the bench.
The cup was full of coffee.
That's why she wanted me to stop.
The cash box was behind the desk.
The cup on the desk was her coffee for her coffee break.

I bought her another coffee. It was the least I could do. She can fish the pound out
of her original one herself. She can give it to the hospice. It's a great cause.

I took the paper too. I figured I might as well. It just cost me about 4 quid.

Sunday, 30 October 2016
I've just picked my wee daughter Emma up from work at Titanic. There are
thousands and thousands of people and children and families and couples there for
the fireworks and the carnival. It's absolutely totally bloody brilliant to see. It's also
very easy to forget that 20 years ago everywhere would have been deserted on this
night.
Now granted it's not ideal to see the like of Peter #imthemayorofclontibret and
Martin #iwasneverintheiraicantevenspellira and rest of the bigot brothers in charge.

his however has resulted in more and more of a normal society for the rest of us. Anyway, long may they keep them locked up arguing in Stormont and let the rest of us get on with it. Evening Belfast. You are looking fabulous this evening.

Thursday, 3 November 2016

There was a fly in the bedroom last night.
I was trying to read my book and he was buzzing around and dive bombing the lamp.
He was doing my head in and I couldn't concentrate on the book.
I tried to swat him with the book but I wasn't fast enough.
I turned off the lamp and opened the bathroom door and turned on the light there.
I stood there waiting for the fly to go towards the light.
He didn't go in.
Then I thought I was maybe blocking the door.
And the fly wouldn't come in.
I got my book and went and sat on the loo well away from the door, keeping an eye on the fly.
I waited and waited.
I sat on the loo chanting come to the light, come to the light.
My mammy would have told me that there is wiser eating grass.
Hells Bells was stirring.
The chant was working.
The fly eventually wandered in to see what the fuss was about. The fly appeared bored.
I dived for the door.
I turned off the light.
I went back to bed.
I turned on the lamp.
I got snug and settled and cosy.
I reached for my book.
My book wasn't there.
I had left the book in the bathroom with the fly.
I would have to leave it.
There was no way was i going to risk letting the fly back out after all that.
I told the Hells Bells to shut up about the light and I tried to sleep.
The fly won. I still couldn't sleep.

Tuesday, 8 November 2016

I'm in the good books.
It has been known before, but not very often.
And it's all down to X Factor.
And Robbie Williams.

Robbie sang his new song.
It's called I love my life.
It goes like this.
I love my life, I am powerful, I am beautiful, other banal shite etc.
But I misheard.
I wasn't really listening.
It's a man thing not to really listen.
I thought he sang I love my wife.
So I sang along.
And I made the rest of the words to suit.
I love my wife, she is powerful, she is beautiful. other banal shite, etc.
So now I'm in the good books.
It's nice.
I must try to visit more often.
Thanks for the help Robbie

Friday, 11 November 2016
I've got a nice clean car. Do you want to know why?

My car was absolutely filthy earlier. There is building work out the lane and we ar
driving through muck and mess going in and out. I was in Papa Browns restaurant
at lunchtime, but the car park was full, so I had to park on the street. I got a space
between the Euro car wash and the bookies. I parked there in my dirty car and in
for lunch I went.

I finished 40 mins later, and out I went. As I was walking back to the car I noticed
how clean it was on the side facing me. It was looking flash. It was gleaming. The
alloys were shining. The chrome was bright and clear. I thought to myself what a
fine-looking car I have.

I went around to the driver's side to get in. That side was filthy. The wheels were
covered in muck and the chrome was dull and dirty. I stood puzzled inspecting the
car, and how half of it was gleaming, while the other half was filthy. I was
wondering if wind direction and driving rain could cause such a phenomenon.

It was only then that I noticed the giggling heads peeking out the door of Euro car
wash. While I was in Papa Browns the workers had stretched over the hose and
cleaned the side of the cars closest to them. They did the car in front of me. They
did the car behind me too. All three cars between the car wash and the bookies
were spotless on one side.

I climbed in.
They watched me.

started the engine.
They watched me.
I drove out of the parking space.
They watched me.
I turned into their yard.
They cheered and whooped and high fived and ran out of the shed to take their stations and do the other side.

That my friends is why my car is spotless. Both sides.

Monday, 14 November 2016

It's a cold day. I was driving back from Carrick this morning. I turned into Irish Quarter South. This took me past the Euro car wash. The car is dirty again. Two of the washers of undeterminable gender were standing leaning against the wall. Wrapped up well against the cold. When they saw me turning in the road they stood up and nudged each other and waved. I beeped and waved back. They beckoned me in. Suggestively. Pleadingly. Imploringly. I shook my head and pointed at my watch. They gave me the sad faces. I gave them the sure what are you going to do shrug. And I drove on past.

I now feel guilty ☐☐.

Monday, 14 November 2016

Quick question lads.
You see Donald Trump's wall?
Is it to keep the Mexicans out?
Or to keep the Americans in?

Wednesday, 30 November 2016

Two glass of prosecco.
Two bags of southern Tayto.
For the Hells Bells and me.
I don't often do romance, but when I do, I do it right.

Friday, 2 December 2016

Wee daughter Emma went out with the mates the other night. I was a wee bit miffed because she was just out of hospital and needed to rest, recuperate and relax.
Where were u says me?
Abbeycentre she says.
For a coffee she says.

I was a wee bit miffed because we are tea people, not coffee people.
Who with says me.
She replied with a boys name.
Just the two of you says me.
Aye she says.
I was a wee bit miffed because there are hundreds of varieties of coffee like
Cappuccino and Frappuccino and decaf and latte and all that shite and it's all very
complicated for coffee drinkers to decide what they want, then order what they
want, then get what they want made, then pay for what they wanted, while I'm
stuck behind them in the queue waiting for a tea, but tea is tea is tea. And we are
tea people.
What did you have says me?
Nothing says she, but he had tea.
I was a wee bit miffed because she had said a boy's name and I hadn't realised at
first, I was so upset at the thought of her being a coffee drinker.
How did he take his tea says me?
Milk in last she says.
I checked she says, all proud of herself.
OK pet says me.
He's a keeper says me.
You treat that nice lad well says me.
He's definitely a keeper says me.
Off she went to bed. Beaming. Delighted. Over the moon. The Hells Bells had a
funny look on her face. She was giving me that 'Really?' questioning look. That
puzzled look. That bemused look. Can't think why. I thought it went well. This
parenting lark is a doddle.

Tuesday, 6 December 2016
You know that term 'went to sleep'? You know that term 'passed'? I never really
understood those terms. I always thought people died. They didn't go to sleep.
They died.

Then 10 years ago man of whom I was very fond went to sleep in my arms. And
then I understood the term. He knew what was happening. He was sad to go but he
didn't fear it. He knew he was just moving on. He knew he was just passing.

Sleep tight Peter Fog. We miss you. For a quiet wee man, you've left a mighty big
hole in our lives.

Thursday, 8 December 2016
My wee daughter Emma couldn't get her car started. I wasn't in the mood to be
distracted, but I had to help. I told her to get the jump leads. I brought my car over

jump start it. I couldn't get the jump leads connected to my battery. I put my car
ck. We pushed her Kia up the drive. We pushed it back down to bump start. It
ouldn't start. We pushed it up again. We pushed it back down. It still wouldn't
art.
old her to call the mechanic. She did. He offered to loan her a booster pack. She
ked me for a lift down. I wasn't in the mood to be distracted, but I had to help.
'e went down and got the booster pack. She opened the bonnet. I connected the
ooster. I stood at the front. She was in the car. I told her to try to start it. She
arted it. While it was still in gear, with no handbrake on. It jumped forward. It
inged my knee. I fell into the engine bay. I could see Emma though the gap
etween the bonnet and the bulkhead, as the engine purred beneath me. She was
oking at me dubiously. Her expression seemed to indicate that while she didn't
ow much about booster packs or car engines, she strongly suspected that me
etting into the engine bay wasn't part of the procedure. My head was at the brake
rvo. My arse was between the headlights. My legs were kicking in the air. The
uilders across the river must have seen me being eaten by a Kia Picanto. Emma
w the funny side as I limped away with oil on my fleece and a bruise on my
nee. I didn't see the funny side. As she was leaving to return the booster pack I
ld her not to turn off the car because the battery was weak.
/hat she says?
on't turn off the car, the battery is weak says me again.
he couldn't hear what I was saying.
o she turned off the car.
just walked away. One of those days.

Monday, 12 December 2016
was invited to a cheeky Nandos in Belfast with the Hells Bells and the wee sister.
hen I got to mind the bags while they went to pee. Then I got to bring the bags
ome so they could shop unladen.
Wee sister mentioned that she was off work today and tomorrow.
laughed at her.
oday is Sunday says me.
ou are always off on Sundays says me.
oday is Monday she replied.
s it? says me.
Really? says me
t is she says.
Really, she says.
thought about it.
Where did Sunday go? says me.
The Hells Bells interjected.
You worked all day she says.
Doing accountancy work she says.

You were all proud of yourself she says.
I was putting up the Christmas decorations she says.
And you worked and hid out of the way she says.
I thought about it.
That was Saturday says me.
No, she says.
Saturday you were dying after your Christmas dinner Friday night she says.
Saturday passed you by she says.

So, I missed Saturday hung over. As a result, I thought Sunday was actually Saturday. And therefore I thought Monday was actually Sunday. If I had thought about it, it would have been slightly odd to have an appointment with a client in East Belfast on a Sunday morning. But I didn't think.

Friday must have been a cracking night!!!

Monday, 19 December 2016
There is a wee street called Mullaghmore Park in Greenisland.
It's a right-angled street, with a private lane going straight ahead at the corner.
The private lane looks like part of the street, but it's not. It's a private lane.
Kenneth Branagh lived there once, he could explain.
Anyway, a man that lived there once parked an old car on the lane while he was having work done.
It was an old Peugeot Estate that hadn't run in years.
It wasn't taxed or insured, and it had to be kept on private property.
Clampers came in and clamped it.
The owner came home from work and saw them.
He parked right opposite the Peugeot Estate, which completely blocked access in or out.
The clampers explained that they had the right to clamp the car, and were going to seize it as it was on a public road, and that the owner would have substantial fees to pay.
The owner didn't bother to explain.
He walked into his shed and took out his angle grinder.
He walked back to the car and proceeded to cut off the clamp.
The clampers gleefully informed him that he had committed criminal damage and that he would be taken to court and prosecuted and there would be even more fees to pay.
The owner informed the clampers that they were on private property, and they would be prosecuted, they would have fees to pay, and he refused to let them leave.
They phoned the office.
The office checked the maps.

The office checked with the police.

The office confirmed that this was indeed private property.

The office phoned the owner to apologise and to ask him to move his van.

The owner said there was a release fee.

The office asked how much.

The owner asked how much their release fee was.

The office said £250.

The owner said funny his release fee was the same.

The office said they would send him a cheque.

The owner asked if they accepted cheques.

The office admitted they didn't.

The owner decided he didn't either.

The office said they would send down cash.

The owner also said that the Peugeot wheel had been damaged.

The office said that this was caused by the removal with the angle grinder.

The owner said that the removal with the angle grinder was caused by the trespassing of their operatives.

The office asked how much the wheel was worth.

The owner gave them the option of finding a scrap man with a wheel from a 30-year-old Peugeot with the same standard of tyre, or they could send him £100.

The office decried the outlandish overcharging, but realised they had no option.

The owner then decided that he wanted something for his trouble.

They settled on a bottle of whiskey for him, and a bunch of flowers for the wife.

The money, the whiskey and the flowers arrive soon after.

The owner moved his van and allowed the clampers to leave.

He left the Peugeot there. He hoped they would come back again. They never did.

Monday, 26 December 2016

Me mammy is coming North for her St Stephens day dinner. The Hells Bells is here preparing a Boxing day dinner. It's going to be a balancing act here, even though both dinners are technically the same. I'm walking a knife edge. This across the barricades stuff is tricky.

Anyway, happy St Stephens day, or Boxing day if you are that way minded.

Friday, 30 December 2016

I got the car washed this morning. But it appears that my friends, the illegal immigrants, have illegally emigrated. And the new illegal immigrants don't know this legal immigrants funny wee ways.

The wash wasn't good. The washer wanted me to move forward a foot to finish the wheels. I was engrossed in my phone. He rapped on the window and frightened me. I jumped. He laughed.

He finished the wheels. I went back to my phone. He wanted me to move to the drying section. I was engrossed. He rapped on the window again. He frightened me again. I jumped again. He laughed again.

The good-looking money taking tip earning girl came to do the polishing. She dried off the car. I opened the window to pay her, so that she couldn't rap on it and frighten me again. She worked her way around the car. She didn't notice the window open. I didn't notice the spray of window cleaner until it landed on my lap. Needless to say, it frightened me.

I paid her. She paused a second for a tip. I paused a second thinking she was giving me some money back for frightening me. I'm never going back there. I miss my normal illegal immigrants. I don't like these new ones. My lap is sticky.

Saturday, 31 December 2016
I love this time of night. The kids are in and home and in bed. The friends have left us with memories and giggling and laughter. The house slowly cools down and ticks quietly to sleep. The neighbours across the river have one by one turned the lights off, the smokers have had a last puff, they have gone inside and settled down for the night. The gurgling of the river seems to quieten down for the night. We will all do it all again tomorrow, but for now everyone is home snug and safe and sound. I'm going to give the kids a hug tomorrow. Call the auld doll. Say hello. Remind myself how lucky I am. Family. Friends. What more do we really need? Night ya headers. You are worse than me for reading this sentimental shite. Cu tomorrow. □□

Friday, 20 January 2017
I had cause to be at A&E in Antrim the other night. It was some shambles. It was some shambles because places like Larne Carrick and Whiteabbey have closed their A&E departments while more and more houses have been built in the areas. And everyone ends up in Antrim. So, there I was.

There was a bad car accident. Two kids were rushed in. There was another car accident. Six people came in ambulances.

A doctor went to all the waiting areas. He seemed to be on the very edge of panic. He explained that they had just saved two lives, were working on 6 more, and would see everyone there eventually, but if it wasn't urgent could they please go

...ome. The nurses were astonished. They had never seen a doctor do that before. ...ome people left without complaining. Some people left while complaining. We ...ayed.

...here was a man sitting at right angles straight in front of me. He was loudly and ...rsistently upset and complaining. He had gone to the GP to get his sick line and ...ere was a locum GP who sent him to hospital for tests when he has been on the ...ck for 15 years and knows more about medicine than any GP straight of school ...d this was a terrible thing to do to a man on the sick 15 years and he had 2 dogs ...home in the kitchen that need walked 2 miles every morning and 2 miles every ...ening and he should have only been gone half an hour and they would be thirsty ...d hungry and this is a massive insult to a man on the sick for 15 years and all he ...eds is a sick line and he doesn't want any of those foreign bloody doctors they ...n't have a clue and he can't understand them anyway and he pays their feckin ...ages anyway with his taxes and they make him wait and him and poor man on ...e sick 15 years with 2 dogs in the kitchen needing walked and fed. I ignored him. ...'e all ignored him. I wanted to tell him that if he could walk 2 miles every ...orning and 2 miles every evening then he was well fit to work and shouldn't be ...n the sick. I wanted to tell him as he was living on benefits he doesn't pay tax, ...d he certainly doesn't pay for any foreign doctors. But I didn't say anything.

...priest sauntered in. With that priestly walk. And the priestly sympathetic eyes. ...'ell-practiced in the art of consoling. Howaye Father. The nurses knew exactly ...here to send him.

...here is a wee pensioner behind 15 year sick man. She has a big lump sticking out ...f her ankle. She is with her granddaughter. Granddaughter thinks they have been ...orgotten. Granny says they will soon remember. Granddaughter wants to go and ...heck. Granny says no, leave them be, she is grand.

... wee young doctor walked past. I have never ever ever ever seen anyone as tired ...s that wee doctor.

...eople were getting called in and out. Minor injuries dealt with. Every seat was ...aken in waiting. Every bed was full. Every trolley was taken in the hall. Still we ...vaited.

...he priest left. He was clutching his bible and rosary beads. He wasn't sauntering. ...lead down. He looked 10 years older. Greyer. Paler. It looked his faith had taken a ...attering.

...went out to get a drink. There was a paramedic ahead of me in the queue. A ...eceptionist was asking him why was he not gone home, his shift finished hours ...go. He said he went home. He said he sat down. He said he had brought the 2 kids in hours earlier after the car accident. He said he couldn't stay at home thinking and praying. So, he came back in to sit and wait for any news. When I went back to m seat she had taken him to wait behind the reception desk.

15 years on the sick man got seen. He got released. He didn't get a sick line, he needed more tests. He walked away leaving his drinks bottle and his snack wrappers lying there. I got up and put them in the bin, so other people could sit down. It was exactly 9 feet away. I measured it. He was just going out the door, as I said loudly 'hope those dogs have crapped all over your kitchen'. I hope he heard The kids beside me thought this was funny, their mum didn't.

It's just not fair lads. The pressure that is put on the medical people here is just not fair. We are taking some of the most caring sympathetic people we have and treating them badly. That pressure they are working under is wrong.

The wee granny got called, she limped badly as she went in. We got called and treated. The two kids Mary and Fintan are still hanging on to life this morning as I write this.

Thursday, 26 January 2017
I was on the phone to Her Majesty's Revenue and Customs. I got through to a lovely Welsh lady, ever so plummy and proper and polite. We went through the security questions. Name address date of birth etc. I passed security. I got the information I needed. Then she said to me, completely out of the blue, I love your accent.
Thanks, says me, I've had it from I was a child.
Oh she giggled, you Irish are so funny.
Well says me, I actually like your accent too.
Thank you she says.
And then her voice went into a whisper, she moved closer to the phone, you know how you just know that someone is holding their hand over the mouthpiece so as not to be overheard.
Elocution she whispered.
3 years' worth she whispered.
So I could better myself she whispered.
Mummy insisted she whispered.
Well done mummy says me.
The elocution worked says me.
Why thank you kind sir she says in a flirty whisper.
Is that all I can do for you Sir she says, heavily breathing down the phone.
I moved closer to my phone. I shielded the handset with my hand.
It is, thanks, sorry I didn't get your name I whispered.

...don't know why I'm whispering, I'm on my own here. It seems like the thing to ...

...he giggled.

...eanor she replied.

...shivered. I didn't even say goodbye. I just put the phone down. My wife is an ...eanor with an accent, I couldn't cope with another one.

Monday, 6 February 2017

...m thinking about living in Northern Ireland. I'm thinking about my kids. I'm ...inking about their future. I'm thinking about the politicians. I'm thinking about ...ow far we have come. I'm thinking about how far we have to go. And I'm ...ustrated. I'm disappointed. Our local school has had to lay off staff despite ...creasing numbers. The politicians have returned millions of the Education budget ...ecause they can't agree when or how to use it. So, I'm going to share my thoughts.

...he Shinners want enquiries into every murder by the British, while refusing to ...release any information about their own activities. Not for me lads. All in or none ...l. Either all information about all murders in the public domain, or draw a line and ...move on. All victims are equal. The Shinners also want to foist Irish on everyone ...or everyday use. I'm not a fan of this. Irish is one of the most wonderful lyrical ...lting rolling poetic languages in the world. It's the language of love and romance ...nd shifting and dreaming and yarning and heroism and worship with a healthy ...isrespect for authority. It's not the language for court proceedings or bin ...ollections in Upper Falls. Not for me lads. Irish or Ulster Scots shouldn't be ...oisted or forced. It should drift in and out as need be. In the place-names and the ...icknames and the myths and legends. Leave the rest of it in the language of ...ommerce and business. Leave it in English.

...he DUP meanwhile are anti everything. Even where they are pro something, they ...re so thran and gurny that we are never quite sure (gurny and thran are brilliant ...Ulster Scots words) (see above). An awful lot of things they do appear at first ...lance to be slightly one sided. And at second glance very one sided. We all accept ...hey will have pro Protestant values. Grand. We accept that they won't be great ...raic at a party. Grand. We accept they will be tight as a Cavan man. Grand. We ...vill not accept them having antiquated anti-Catholic anti-gay or anti-everything ...alues any more. We will not accept the friends and family that dived into the ...rough of RHI. Trying to remove a miniscule £50k grant to take kids to the ...Gaeltacht to learn Irish? Not for me lads. Besides the kids don't go to the Gaeltacht ...o learn Irish. The Gaeltacht isn't about Irish or Nationalism or any other isms. ...Kids go looking for the shift. No other reason. Be pro prod. Everyone will accept ...hat. Try not to be so anti everything else. We won't accept that.

Anyway, we voted for peace, equality, parity of esteem. But we are not seeing it. Our politicians should be drifting to a central position of acceptance and tolerance not pandering to the extremists who deal drugs for Ulster or smuggle diesel for Ireland. The Northern Ireland football and boxing fans have made new friends all over the world, dancing and singing their way round Europe and USA. The Ulster fans sang the Fields of Athenry in Ravenhill in respect. The Irish fans sang Stand up for the Ulster man in respect. Most of us normal people have moved miles. So why the feck are we having to drag our politicians with us? Why aren't they leading?

Maybe someday we will see efforts towards this. Maybe we will see street signs telling us when we are leaving a town, any town, any county, and wishing us Safe Home, Slan Abhaile, Haste ye back. Lovely phrases. All traditions respected. Equality. Parity. Maybe someday on occasion we can see a flag flying over civic buildings which is representative of everyone and agreeable to all in NI. Maybe we will hear the same anthem sung proudly equally at home in Windsor and in Casement. For Northern Ireland. By Northern Ireland. In Northern Ireland. Maybe our politicians will work towards this.

Or maybe they won't. I'm going to mix Northern and Southern Tayto for a snack. Parity. Equality. Give and take.

Tuesday, 7 February 2017
It's my birthday. Big son took me out for my breakfast before he heads to Coleraine and I head to Belfast. I settled on Springsteen's because it's my birthday. The wee waitress came over.
What can I get you she says?
Tea please says me.
She makes a sad sympathetic face.
No tea she says.
Sorry? says me.
No tea. Boiler is broken she says.
David tell her how much I love tea says me to David.
He does says David to her.
I do says me to her.
He does says David to her again.
Boiler is broken she says to me.
No tea she says to David and me.
I wanted to tell her it's my birthday. I wanted to tell her that I like tea. I wanted to tell her that I love tea. That I can't function without tea. That tea makes me fertile and alive and rampant and eloquent and lyrical and musical and surprisingly attractive to women with natural eyebrows. But I didn't.
Orange juice please says me sadly.

Tuesday, 14 February 2017

Came out of a client's offices on Shore road Belfast. There is a wee residential home for the disabled behind it. There is a bus sitting at the pavement and a young lady is walking some residents to the bus. The footpath is blocked. I could push my way through but I stand and wait. It seems polite. I stand there waiting and nodding the people, while holding my briefcase and a big box of books.

Morning sir says me to a gentleman just getting on the bus.

He stopped.

One foot on the steps.

He turned around.

Morning he replied with a big genuine unashamed happy smile.

I thought that had gone well so I did it again.

Morning Sir says me to the gentleman following behind him.

Is that a present for your girlfriend he says to me, nodding at the box.

They all laughed.

Yeah says me, but don't tell the wife.

They all roar. All in good form.

Where you all off to? says me to the next passenger, a middle-aged lady.

To the park, she says.

Grand day for it says me.

Aye she says, not like last week. Last week was feckin freezing.

I burst out laughing. Couldn't help it. It was so unexpected.

The passengers all roar.

The driver grins. He likes his job. You can tell.

The assistant doesn't grin. But she wants to. She likes her job too. You can tell.

Behave yourself Betty she warns.

I laughed harder.

We call my wife Betty sometimes too I tell them. She swears like a feckin trooper too.

This time the assistant joins in the laughter.

Uproar on the bus. Off I go to my car, carrying the briefcase and the books, tears in my eyes laughing. They go past in the bus as I'm putting the books in the boot. They beep and wave and bounce and cheer. I wave and give the thumbs up back. I keep waving until they are out of sight. I've made some new friends. I wish I could go to the park with them.

Nice start to the day.

Thursday, 16 February 2017

Anyway gentlemen it appears that every female in Carrick is at the cinema tonight watching the 50 Shades movie with Jamie Dornan.

We need to be prepared for the onslaught gentlemen.
Remember the first movie gentlemen.
They will pour out in a fervent rampant heightened state at 11pm, full of vim, vigour, prosecco, jelly babies and hormones.
We need to exercise caution gentlemen.
There are no rules on chemical weapons in this battle.
Chilli and garlic tuna and raw onion sandwiches.
Cheese and onion crisps as a further deterrent.
This is a defensive action gentlemen.
Do not get suckered into a counterattack.
Do not get isolated and alone.
These ladies will pounce and show no mercy to stragglers.
Guard your manhole at all times.
Do not charge their fox holes.
Beware of the booby traps.
Good luck gentlemen.

Monday, 20 February 2017
I'm at the MOT centre in Larne. I did my motorbike test here many years ago. We came past the port, me on my wee Suzuki 125 Marauder with 40k on the clock, the instructor on a big cruiser, and then a Woodside Haulage car transporter behind us. We went right at the roundabout heading up the carriageway towards KFC. The Woodside lorry moved into the fast lane. I reckoned that if I could keep alongside the lorry through the next roundabout then I would miss the exit on the right up the town. The next exit off the carriageway was at the driving test place and the instructor wouldn't make me go the whole way back down into the town. So I floored it.
Woodside driver was being very nice and trying very hard to get out of my way. I trying to keep Woodside driver in my way. The wee bike gave me everything it had. It wasn't much. We came past KFC into the roundabout, I braked later than Woodside man, and gained half a lorry length. I sat straight up to brake, rear tyre skipping, left knee out, left knee down, kiss the apex, head down, arse up, lean right, right knee down, kiss the apex, on the power, quick flip left, kiss the apex again and power up the hill. He had more power than me, I had 8hp between my legs and I wasn't scared to use it.
Off we went up the hill.
Woodside started gaining.
His exhaust was choking me.
I was getting spattered with grit.
The vibration was rattling my fillings.
The heat was burning my legs.
I glanced in my mirror.
The instructor was indicating.

still had it planted.
didn't change gear.
The instructor moved right.
one missed change and it was all over.
waited for the instructor to tell me to slow down.
e was still in the outer lane behind the lorry.
was at 8 thousand revs in second gear, engine roaring, tyres squealing, blood pumping, teeth grinding, eyes rattling.
was now a drag race.
His superior horsepower was telling.
His trailer wheels were beside me, then in front of me, then moving into the distance.
glanced right.
saw the turning lane two lanes over.
waited for the instruction.
The radio crackled.
think we have missed our exit the instructor says.
We will go on back to the centre he says.
smiled to myself.
relaxed.
changed gear because the engine was still roaring.
went for third and ended up in first.
The engine gave an almighty scream.
Huge puff of smoke.
took a massive wobble but just held it.
back into third, and up the carriageway back to the centre. Congratulations he says. You've passed he says. Only one minor he says. For the missed gear change on the carriageway he says. I felt like arguing. I felt like telling him that I wasn't safe on the roads and that no way should I be allowed out. But then I reckoned that not even Joey Dunlop would have gone through that roundabout as quick with a forty foot Woodside lorry beside him. So I took the accolade. And that is how to pass a motorbike test in Larne. Thanks for the help Woodside Haulage.

Tuesday, 21 February 2017

My wee daughter came in to say bye.
She was dressed smartly in her professional coat. Hair set, nails painted and make up done. I looked at her and wondered sadly how she had suddenly got so grown up. She said she was off to university in Coleraine and she would see me Friday. And I thought sadly about how she is a young lady now. I asked if she was getting the train, no she said she was driving. And I thought proudly but sadly that she is an independent sophisticated young lady getting on with her own wee life driving her own wee car and living in her own wee flat.

And then she showed me the wee teddy bear in her professional dressy coat pocket to keep her company all week in her wee flat. And I was happier. Because underneath it all she is still daddy's wee girl. Bye pet. Ya wee header.

Monday, 27 February 2017
You want to go for a walk he says.
Aye, I will pick you up says me.
Will we walk up the hill he says.
No says me, the hills kill me.
Will we walk down the hill he says.
No says me because then we will only have to walk back up.
Will we park at the castle and walk he says.
Grand says me.
So we did.
We walked to Fisherman's Quay.
We crossed the road.
We walked over the railway bridge.
We walked back past the Leisure Centre.
Will we go up North road he says.
No says me, the hills kill me.
Will we go back to the car he says.
No says me, it's too early.
Where do you want to go he says.
For a pint says me.
So we did.
We put the world to rights, and sorted out Stormont over the pint.
Will we walk on out past the marina and back he says.
We have another pint while we decide says me.
So we did.
And we put the world back out of sync, and bolloxed up Stormont. We finished the pint.
Then we went home.
This exercise is fierce hard work. It's driving me to drink.

Wednesday, 1 March 2017
There is a wee adult centre on Irish Quarter West. It's part of Hawthorns adult centre for adults that struggle with everyday life. It's on the right, beside where Caters used to be. Before the YMCA. That's the spot.

They have a pool table and the TV and they sit and socialise and play games and stuff and chat. They have big windows on a corner site so they can see a good bit down the road. Anyway, every time I go past I give a beep and a wave because I

now quite a few of them, and they all wave back at me, and they enjoy it, and
they always say to me 'saw you the other day' when I meet them, and i say 'saw u
back' and now lots of the rest of them that I don't know wave at me in Carrick
because they recognise the car from beeping at them. And I do it because they love
it. And it's only a beep beep and a wave to me. I barely slow down. But it means a
lot to them.

Anyway this morning I went down Irish Quarter and I got ready to beep beep and
wave. I put down the window and put my right arm out and held my left hand over
the horn while steering with my knees. But there was no one there to wave back at
me. The room was empty.

I was sad. So there you go. It appears that instead of beeping at them because it
makes them happy, I'm actually beeping at them because it makes me happy. And
maybe they are sitting inside wonder who the eejit is beeping and waving on the
way past. And maybe they decide to wave back because I seem to like it. Maybe
they talk about me.

There's that eejit again.
Beeping and waving.
Ah God love him, he's not quite right.
The bin lorry doesn't go the whole way up that street.
Jaysus he's going to kill someone.
Better wave at him.
He seems to like it.
Feckin eejit.

I'm going to keep waving. And beeping. I'm going round past it again now. To see
if they are back. Feckin eejits the lot of us.

Friday, 17 March 2017
Have you the car packed for Fermanagh for the weekend says me.
Aye love she says.
Did you get it all in says me?
Aye love she says.
Tight fit says me?
No love she says.
Room for some tools says me?
Aye love she says.
Room for the golf clubs says me?
Are they clean she says?
Hmmmmm says me.
No, she says.
Not a hope she says.

Not going to happen she says.
Cars full she says.
Couldn't squeeze anything more in she says.
Loaded she says.
Overweight she says.

I should have packed the car myself. I will know in future. 🙂🙂

Wednesday, 22 March 2017
I was driving down the road with the wee daughter.
Just the 2 of us.
The radio was on.
Caravan of Love by the Housemartins.
We sang along.
She knew every word.
I was impressed.

Daaaadddd she says questioningly. She didn't look at me. She kept looking out the
passenger window.
Yes pet says me.
That's your song she says.
Is it says me.
Aye you always sing that song she says.
On occasion i suppose says me.
But it's a real song she says.
Course it's a real song says me, puzzled.
On the radio, she says.
I know says me, even more puzzled.
But I thought it was just one of those stupid wee songs you make up to drive mum
mad when we are going to the caravan she says.
No pet it's a real song says me.
Off the radio says me.
Driving your mum mad is just a bonus says me.

And we drove down the road singing our hearts out and happy. I was happy
because I was with my wee girl. I was happy because she thought I had written a
massive chart hit. I was happy because the Housemartins were driving her mum
mad. She was happy because she knows she can twist her old dad round her little
finger.

So I sang Stand up. And she sang Stand up. And we harmonised for the final Stand
up with the key change in the final up.

he next song was Timber by a nice young chap called Mr Pete Bull who kept
lling down and yelling timber. Sounds like early onset of Parkinson's to me. I
dn't a clue what Mr Pete Bull were on about. I didn't sing along.

riday, 24 March 2017
was up at the skips in Carrick. Trailer load of stuff. Mixed waste. Two lads there
orking were leaning on the general waste compactor.
here does this go lads says me?
ver there they grunted.
yres says me?
on't take them they grunted.
hen a young lady in a jeep came in. Out she climbed. Wearing training pants.
ants that left very little to the imagination. She started to take out her rubbish. The
vo lads almost sprinted over. Carl Lewis and Ben Johnson.
ll right love.
will take that.
ind your hands there love.
eave that wood over there love and I will bring it through.
hat all ya have love.
hat's grand love, thanks for coming up.
ee you again.
ake care.
ye bye b b b bye. Bye. Bye.

found a bit of wood at the bottom of the trailer. I left it beside pants girls wood.
a can't leave that there grunted Carl.
h OK says me.
went to walk through to the timber recycling in the ajoining yard.
ou can't go through there grunted Ben, you have to drive.
h OK says me.
)ff I went driving the 40 yards to the timber recycling.
heers lads says me.
hey didn't look up. They didn't reply.
ye then says me.
othing.
ext time I'm at the skips I'm going to wear training pants that leave very little to
he imagination. See how Ben and Carl like that.

unday, 26 March 2017
went to the Novena held by Fr Brian D'Arcy in the Graan monastery in
nniskillen. It is to be his last novena, he is sadly moving on. Jim Breen from
ycle Against Suicide was the guest speaker.

In honour of Jim I cycled from the caravan round to the Graan. In the Cycle Against Suicide colours. Up the drive into the monastery. All the cars were parked side by side filling the car park like they were going on the ferry to Scotland. I thought it would be a laugh to cycle behind the cars right up in the very middle and stand there like an eejit. The helpers didn't bat an eyelid.

I suppose it is Fermanagh.

Those sorts of things happen in Fermanagh.

We stood outside the chapel to wait for others. It was 10.30. The helpers welcomed us and told us to go on in. It wasn't to start until 11, but Fr Brian started when Fr Brian wanted. In we went, to the back row. Myself, Hells Bells, Jo and Pete, all keeping the colours flying. Fr Brian said hello. It was 10.40. He asked where everyone was from. He went through the counties. Some were from Kilkenny. He asked where they stayed. They named the townland.

He seemed puzzled.

Who are you staying out there with he says.

We all laughed.

John and Mary came the reply.

Aw John and Mary, they are lovely he says.

Was the breakfast good he says?

We laughed again.

The Kilkenny people assured him it was.

Fr Brian wasn't surprised. John and Mary were related to Derek Ryan's management ya see. Apparently that guarantees a good breakfast. Anyone from further away he asked.

Croydon came the reply from the right.

Ooohhh Croydon Fr Brian repeated.

How posh he says.

We laughed again. We gave the Croydon lads a round of applause. This was more like a chat than a novena. It was all very relaxed and chilled and welcoming. Fr Brian told us to go to the shop before we leave. It's round the other side. He hasn't been pushing it enough lately. So please visit the shop before we go. We decided we would.

He started the novena. The music was so good it was unbelievable. The speeches were spellbinding and uplifting and funny and sad and just absolutely bloody amazing.

Can you reach higher? Do you feel bigger?

I could. I did.

Communion time came all too soon. Fr Brian only had five helpers at communion. He discussed it with the congregation. He felt he needed more. The congregation concurred. He put out the call. People pounced from everywhere all round pulling chalices out of jackets and handbags. He ended up with twelve. Now we've too many he says. The congregation concurred. He decided to go with it.

waited for him to pick his spot. I'm not a fan of lay minsters. I prefer to deal with
the main man. I told the Hells Bells where I was going. Especially as it was his last
novena. I ducked past the lay minister beside me. I hope that's not a sin. If it is I
hope it's only a venial sin and not a mortal sin. I stood in the queue for Fr Brian in
my cycling tights and my bright orange rain jacket. We shuffled forward. Everyone
else was only 5 feet tall so I had a great view. The right-hand queue was empty.
The female lay minister on that side gave me the nod. Cmon ahead big lad nod. I
stayed where I'm was for Fr Brian.

Onward we shuffled.
Then he ran out of communion.
There were still two in front of me.
I thought he would have taken the lay ministers chalice to finish off.
He didn't.
Off he went.
The lay minister stepped in.
She gave a holy pious devout gotcha ya bollox smile to me.
I thought you were too good for me smirk.
I took the communion.
I was tempted to decline, but having already committed one sin on the way up I
didn't want to risk condemning my soul to eternal damnation.
I walked back down in disappointment and failure. The Hells Bells couldn't look at
me for laughing. Neither could the lay minister at the back. The novena finished.
Fr Brian dispensed with the final blessing. He told us to clear off to the shop and
spend some money. So we did.

We met him on the way out. I thanked him for having us. He invited us upstairs for
soup and buns. I wondered if they were they from John and Mary. I think he
thought I had escaped from a wee gated community somewhere, with me tights
and me orange jacket. I desperately wanted a selfie. I didn't like to ask. The church
is against selfie abuse. We declined both the soup and buns, but appreciated the
offer. We didn't bother with the shop. Fairly sure that was not a sin.

I got back on the bike. I left the monastery. Down the drive. Big queue out the
gate. Car car bus car car jeep car orangeeejitonabike car car. We went to the golf
club for chicken and chips. I got a lift home. No more cycling for me. I was
emotionally and spiritually knackered. And full of chicken and chips.
Did I find God?
No.
Did God find me?
I will let you know.
But I'm going to the Novena next year. On the bike. It's gas craic. God bless.

Wednesday, 29 March 2017

Wee daughter phoned me. I saw the name on the phone. I was immediately worried. Worrying is a daddy thing.

Omg the car broke down.

Omg she crashed.

Omg she is hurt.

Omg she will slap me for saying Omg.

Hello Emma says me nervously.

Hi dad, are you in Carrick she chirped

Aye says me.

You want to do breakfast she says.

Aye says me.

I was delighted. Over the moon. Getting to spend time with wee daughter in a social setting is a rare treat. We went for breakfast. She ordered. Sausage beans toast. I went for just tea. I couldn't stop grinning. She was looking at me strangely

This is nice says me with a self-satisfied smirk.

Aye she says through a mouthful of beans.

Thanks for phoning me says me grinning happily.

Well, she says while munching on toast, David didn't answer his phone.

My smirk became less pronounced.

And, she says while wiping up bean sauce, Granny Lily was busy.

My smile disappeared.

Then, she says while putting her knife and fork back on her plate, mum is at work

My smile became a frown.

So, she says I thought I would ask you.

She leaned back.

She burped.

I'm going to head on she says.

Could you get the bill Daddy she says?

Thanks Daddy she says.

Love you Daddy she says.

Bye Daddy she says.

And off she went.

Completely oblivious to the change in my mood.

But stuff it.

Half an hour to spend having a sneaky breakfast with my wee girl?

I will take it.

Anytime.

21192187R00071

Printed in Great Britain
by Amazon